SUBMISSION
to
GLORY

Living a Life That Glorifies God

TRISH PENNALA

WESTBOW
PRESS®
A DIVISION OF THOMAS NELSON
& ZONDERVAN

This book is dedicated
to everyone around the world who,
like Jesus Christ, desires to glorify God.
To all of those who seek the presence of God.

FOREWORD

Now sensibly, we all may "say" that any notion of superiority on the part of one ethnic group or race over another is but an example of the "fall of man" at its worse. Perhaps we need to be reminded that, as Christians, we have been given both a mandate by God's Word and the gift of His grace in Christ to be otherwise. In short, we are called upon to expose this evil, to combat it with Christian charity and kindness, and to diligently work toward providing the only certain "cure" with the gospel of Christ. He has called us to be as salt and light, so that every decision we make and every action we take might be with the intention of making Him known around the world.

The word "submission" is not a word authors throw around because it is popular, but it is the word that Trish Pennala uses to describe the journey of grace, discovery, and growth in our walk of faith in Christ. And, in this sense, it is a perfect word, for even God's grace is only received by us as an act of submission, an admission of our need for God.

By beautifully and systematically pointing this out in each area of life's relationships, Trish takes us down the path of God's plan—His "sacred harmony" as she puts it.

So that, for the person ready to learn the ways of God for real life, I could not commend anything more helpful. Trish shares the truth from God's Word, a perspective that is both refreshing and needed in our world of moral relativism.

By illustrating from a variety of experience—political, corporate, and social—Trish reminds us that all men, women, leaders, and servants must ultimately submit first to God, then to one another, in the order designed by Him to find what it is we most seek: His Glory.

Sam Dennis
Pastor Emeritus
Parkway Hills Baptist Church
Plano, Texas
www.samdennis.net

Recently, it was my good fortune to be asked to review the book you are now holding, *Submission to Glory*, by Trish Pennala. The book was a timely reminder to me about allowing God to work His will for my life in His timing and in His ways.

I encourage you to carefully and prayerfully read this work, allowing God to reclaim the throne of your heart.

In the daily struggle of life, our flesh wars to be in complete control of our life course, often impatiently demanding that God provide answers to our every question and disappointment.

Allow the insights you will gain from reading *Submission to Glory* to once again orient your life in proper alignment with the Trinity. In doing so, you will again know how the joy that lives in the Christian heart, which abides in perfect submission to God.

Mark Ponder
Deacon/Life Group Teacher
First Baptist Church
Carrollton, Texas

ACKNOWLEDGMENTS

Special thanks to:

To Sam Dennis, pastor emeritus, Parkway Hills Baptist Church in Plano Texas: Thanks for showing your dedication to Christ and for expressing your life-changing words to all of us.

To my husband, Brian Pennala: You are to me a gift from God. Thanks for your prayers, love, and support of this book and everything in my life. Also, thank you for encouraging me to continue writing and for your patience while I spent countless hours working on this book. My love for you is unending.

My children—Norman Wayne, LaTarsha, Fredericka, and Rogandia (one of my editors)—for being close in my life and for being such loving children whose great potential I live to see as you become warriors for Christ.

To my late mother, Joy Lee Harris, for setting a forty-year example of how to follow Jesus Christ and your constant reminders to pray and keep God first in everything.

To my father, Louis Harris, for all the years of believing in me and constantly reminding me of how talented I am.

Pastor Joel Osteen of Lakewood Church in Houston, Texas, and Pastor John Avant, formerly of First Baptist Church of West Monroe, Louisiana: Listening to your sermons gave me spiritual guidance, encouragement, and a sense of new direction in life.

INTRODUCTION

Not many of us have the ability to remember the entire details of our childhood. Nor are we able to process the spiritual progression of its growth without mass questions stemming out of confusion. You ask questions, but do you get the absolute answers? The significance of spiritual growth during our childhood is as important as the rest of our life.

Minor crises in life such as disappointments, setbacks, shocks, and regrets are often stored in the forefront of our memory to be opened occasionally. Some sequences of events we call "nonessential" because we feel they are less important. The less important part of our memory is lost. On the contrary, our spirit will always remember these facts.

The big idea behind this book, *Submission to Glory*, is God will to give you answers to the deep cries of your soul. This book will help you to submit your entire life to God. In turn, by giving God the glory, He will give you a better understanding of your place in His kingdom. You will come to see the big picture of God's mission to redeem the world from the hands of Satan. God will show you how important you are to His kingdom and He will reveal how He wants you to participate in His plan.

In my lifetime, I was restricted for many years in seeing God's plan and His greatness for my life because the enemy of God, Satan, had his hands in the development of my spiritual character. I was the one alone, in a room full of people, not wanting people to know I was being tormented. Those days were dark; I knew I was being harassed by Satan, but I didn't know how to ask for help. Even through all that darkness, God found a way for me not to lose sight of Him. I continued to see His shadow as He kept sustaining my life and working in the lives of people around me. God didn't allow me to lose sight of His wonders.

All of our situations and encounters in life are essential to the building and outcome of our character. As we began our journey to adulthood, developing a moral character is vital. Adhering to moral and ethical principles allows our spirit to bring forth its entire memory. In this order, we may be inclined to connect and be in harmony with our creator, the same creator of Heaven and Earth, Jehovah God.

Tapping into our spirit requires peeling back several layers of ourselves. Many layers we didn't even know were there. Uncovering ourselves is sometimes painful, but before the day is over, we are in position to recognize a powerful being beyond ourselves, Almighty God. Yielding to the power and greatness of our creator is called *submission*. During this submission, God receives the *glory*.

Have you ever witnessed the power of God or had an opportunity to enjoy His presence? It's an awesome experience. We all desire to see the wonders and greatness of the Lord. God desires to give each of us knowledge and wisdom through His Word. Jesus Christ is the beloved Son of the creator of the universe, Jehovah God. While on Earth, Jesus was a virtuoso in His walk with God. He was knowledgeable and wise. He has provided us with the greatness example of how to tap into God's greatness and recognize the powers of God at work.

In reading this book, I pray that you will benefit deeply and come to a more perfect union with God. I pray you will encounter the same visions I had which gave me the courage to write on this subject. May you be transformed as I was by witnessing the power of God. On this spiritual journey, may God give you daily peace and a knowledge of His statements concerning submission. I hope you rely on God and trust Him to put you in position to receive all that he has for you. When you finish this book, you will have a deeper knowledge of God's plan for humankind.

John Chapter 1 tells us that Jesus was present from the beginning of creation. From the beginning, Jesus has humbly submitted Himself to His Heavenly Father and today, He is still under submission to God. Consequently, Jesus will forever witness the greatness and glory of the Almighty One, Jehovah God. He is forever bringing forth glory to God's holy name and today we have an opportunity to do the same.

Jehovah is the Supreme Being, the true God of the Holy Bible. This name is understood to mean "He causes to become." Jehovah is the creator of all things, including Heaven and Earth. The name "Jehovah" is God's unique name revealed to us in the Holy Bible. It is the proper name for the God of Israel. He is the God of Abraham, Isaac, and Jacob. In most mainstream English translations of the Bible, the term "Lord" is used, meaning Jehovah.

> *"And I appeared unto Abraham, unto Isaac, and unto Jacob, by the name of God Almighty, but by my name JEHOVAH was I not known to them." (Exodus 6:3, KJV)*

Many years ago, the prophet Isaiah described the greatness of our Heavenly Father to you and me in the Bible. He wrote, *"The glory of the Lord shall be revealed, and all flesh shall see it together, for the mouth of the Lord has spoken"* (Isaiah 40:5, ESV).

The Apostle Paul also wrote these words for us, *"I also pray that you will understand the incredible greatness of God's power for us who believe him. This is the same power that raised Christ from the dead and seated him in the place of honor at God's right hand in the heavenly realms"* (Ephesians 1:19-20, NLT).

Let's climb aboard and put on our seatbelts. The seatbelt is the whole armor of God so that you may take your stand against the devil's schemes (*Ephesians 6:11*). Let's take a ride high above the clouds into an area where there is no noise (from other people or aircrafts), no confusion, and no negativity. This is an area dedicated to those who desire to see the greatness of God, to follow His plan, and to experience His power at work in their lives. The journey may get a little bumpy at times, but the swift rescue of our Lord Jesus will keep your ride smoother than anything you've ever experienced.

CONTENTS

CHAPTER 1

REFLECTIONS OF LIFE

It was the beginning of September 1966. The neighborhood had gotten quiet and all the kids hurried home because of what would take place the next day. The park where many children gathered during the summertime was empty. I went home, too. Stood in the living room starring at my new clothes and things that mom had laid out on the sofa for the occasion. Dad called me over to have a seat next to his recliner. One of my brothers smiled and looked on, in anticipation of my wonder. What could Dad possibly want?

He said, "Trish, tomorrow is a big day for all the kids and I want you to be prepared."

My response: "Prepared?"

"Yes, ready for your first day of school."

We went over, again, the alphabets and numbers I had learned over the summer.

Dad then realized I couldn't spell my name without looking at it written on paper. He said, "You have to learn to spell your name before tomorrow."

"Right now?"

"Yes."

After repeated attempts, I still wasn't getting it. So, with the help of my brother, Darrell, they made up a song: "P-A-T, R-I-C, I—A; P-A-T, R-I-C, I—A!" This melody is still going on in my head today. The song was a winner because my first grader teacher was impressed.

Being the middle child in a family can be challenging for a developing child. Certain expectations come with being in this position. As the child grows, for many, this position can possibly pose a difficultly due to certain expectations. It can be especially difficult for this child when confronted with the conception of a much greater responsibility than normal. How can a person maintain normalcy in this lucky position without showing reluctance and struggling with the course of the system? Well, the grace of God must be present and covering every angle of your being. For the lucky one in this spot, the thought alone can create unusual pressures. Feelings associated with these challenges can be overwhelming. The fact that others may be relying on you may render some resistance. You may feel like freezing in time. The expectation comes from many different angles.

At the same time, being the middle child can be stimulating and exciting because you have the opportunity to emulate both older and younger children. The opportunity exists to go from a mature and responsible person with adult-like behavior to one who is small, undeveloped, and follows along with everything.

One of those overwhelming times of responsibility happened the next day at school. It was mid-morning and all the school kids were out for recess. I remember running around the schoolyard, laughing and making new friends. Then the bell rang. Everyone started running, including me. I ran as fast as I could, non-stop. By the time I made it to the front door, my brother Darrell had caught up with me.

My mom opened the door and asked, "Where are you two going?"

My brother explained his teacher saw me running off the campus and shouted to him, "Darrell, is that your little sister? Go catch her!"

He then apologized to Mom that he couldn't catch me. The bell had rung and all I knew, I was supposed to run. No one said which way. This year went by smoothly, after all.

The Sixties were a time when a brand-new house cost about $15,000 and the minimum wage for labor during that time was $1.25 per hour. There were a lot of good things that came out of the Sixties, including civil rights. We had the Ed Sullivan Show, feathering great music from artists like The Beatles and The Jackson Five. It was also a time when Americans felt the shock of the assassination of the thirty-fifth President of the United States of America, John F. Kennedy, and also Martin Luther King, Jr., a clergyman and civil rights leader.

This was an era that followed World War II. Kids would continue to learn about the history of what happened during this era for years to come. By many, it was referred to as the "Golden Age of America" and living the "American Dream" was a reality. Incomes were on the rise and the new use of credit cards allowed Americans to have more flexibility with their spending. During this time, America watched a human being, Neil Armstrong, set foot on the moon in 1969. This gave the world defining moments of history. Watching television became a way of life and it changed the way Americans viewed the world and war.

The Vietnam War was still in action and young men were being drafted into the military. Most of the men went willingly, but there were those who refused to go and ended up enduring jail time. The war started in November 1955 and ended in April 1975. The United States had the largest foreign military presence and fundamentally directed this war from 1965 to 1972. The rest of the country was given updates of the war by radio or television news briefings.

By the time the war was over, a million people had lost their lives, including 60,000 American soldiers. It was the longest war in the United States history. The enemy was hard to identify and the end result: America had failed to achieve its objectives. Many families had lost a loved one to the war.

In some social units around the country, babies were born by the thousands. The babies were later referred to as the "Baby Boomers." Eleven family members living in a small, yet cozy two-bedroom house was also common during the Sixties. The Harris family was no different than the ordinary. A family, which included an amazing couple who loved each other, and their nine baby boomers: five boys and four girls.

We lived our American dream. There was one in the lucky spot: me. I was a six-year-old female smack dab in the middle. In my memory, our house was somewhat small. In our house, the four girls shared one bedroom and the five boys slept in the other room. Mom and Dad made part of the living room as their sleeping quarters. The existing conditions made it close enough for jokes to laugh at and some things to cry about.

Policy and regulations were alive and well living under the same roof. Other tenants were Mr. Frost, Ms. Sunshine, and a few critters. Everybody knew the arrangement that was set up by our parents. Individuals prepared themselves to be in harmony with support of the union. Our father worked long hours, but still provided quality time for church, family fun and games, and also family vacations. As far back as I can remember, our mother was a prayer warrior, always immersing herself in God's Word daily. She kept our family on her prayer list. She's the one that kept the Harris family together.

As children, we had a great deal of exposure to religion. We were introduced by our parents to the Savior of the world, Jesus Christ. Mom and Dad sat us on the floor in a circle as they read the Bible aloud and told biblical stories. We heard of a Savior who became a light to the world two thousand years ago. This is the same savior that walked with God, taught the truth about His Heavenly Father, Jehovah God, to His disciples. This same truth taught to both Jews and Gentiles (the nations). Jesus served (and still serves) as God's spokesman and sets the example in how we are to live our lives according to God's will: a life that will bring glory to God.

The eleven members of my family and people from all over the world would hear of this good news. Jesus' teachings and how He performed miracles and healed the sick had spread far and wide. As the word spread, more and more people began to follow Jesus, and many would benefit from His preaching and have a chance at everlasting life. All believers are then reconnected with God through a relationship with Jesus Christ. See in the Bible book of Luke 2:1-21.

As baby boomers in this small house, hearing the good news was exiting. As we got a little older, we were inclined to study God's Word on our own, first using children's Bibles. When the time came, each child made a personal decision to follow Christ and made a public confession with baptism. We had all become Christians following Jesus. This was another method of providing support to the family structure: by submitting to the order of the things of God. Our parents arranged structure for the household and it consisted primarily of trainings from the Bible. These lessons aligned us to be in submission to God's word.

Helping out the most fragile and vulnerable sibling in the group was a part of being committed to the union. Without the help from others, attaching oneself to the rules was not easy. This was true especially if you were small, undeveloped, and not sure which guidelines were pertinent for you. Following the rules was not always easy.

At this time, everyone in my family had a glorious time and was excited to be a part of the group. Each had important duties to fulfill including Mr. Frost, Ms. Sunshine, and the few critters that all had their moments with the group. Mr. Frost and Ms. Sunshine gave their performances by making unselfish contributions of their warmth and coolness to the structure.

During the wintertime, Mr. Frost provided an icy slip-in-slide, in the front yard, for us to use as a skating rink. Ms. Sunshine showed up every morning with a beam of light peering through the curtains and this gave us a reason to be outside during the summertime. As for the critters, their moments were undesired, especially by the little ones, but their presence was certainly a necessity of life.

The arrangement also provided us little ones with the opportunity to put good behaviors into practice. The behaviors of "acceptance and tolerance" were often attempted because they were life preservers. Without the quality of acceptance, one would suffer a spiritual decline from their heated selfishness, and without tolerance, one would be killed by their own coldness.

First on the list of duties and responsibilities was *love*. Each child was given a bucket to receive love, develop it, and then deliver gallons of it to others. As for the critters, their job was to drag out the frustration of the weaker ones, to some extent proving them to be dissatisfied with the system of things. The irritations usually meant this noteworthy love bucket was, in need of a refill, or this sibling needed to empty it by pouring out love to another person. It was crucial for the little ones to learn how to fill and empty their bucket in a timely manner.

There were obstacles that posed a problem with the fills and refills of the love buckets. Personal traffic jams, known as behavioral issues, were not at bay. The issues stood in the way and presented irritations for many within the union. The behaviors would flare up and set off a domino effect between the groups. At the same time, love and hope were always there to settle any uproar. As long as your bucket didn't remain full or stay empty, you had a chance to continue in relative harmony.

In every situation where there's a fairly large group, structure is most significant and requires steady organization to keep it stabilized. Sometimes, doubt presented an odd impression for some within the group. An unpredictable feeling arises that you are not in your proper position. This uncertainty and fear caused much confusion and the little ones began to shift out of line.

Desperately trying to get back into the correct position, further mistakes were made and by now, we were out of boundary. Even with our parents handing out reminders daily, some of their little ones still ended up in a different spot. These spots were recognized by our parents as unauthorized. The spots were anger, resentment, envy, irritation, jealousy, and sometimes just plain meanness. Our parents immediately intervened.

Training in motion usually helped us to hold our position and remember each responsibility. This type of discipline is what was needed. It allowed the actual performances of love and affection to take the platform. As my siblings and I learned to fill the buckets with love and affection and empty them in a timely fashion, this prepared each us for a genuine show. This was a daily show that would be watched by mankind. What we did at home would reflect us in the world.

During the rehearsals, Mom and Dad received several complaints and questions that were plaguing the minds of the little ones, including the six-year-old holding the lucky spot. Although privileged to be in this lucky spot and excited to have my own bucket, I was confused and had problems understanding the order of things. I wondered, should I take position alongside the four older siblings with the weight of authority on my shoulders? Or, should I stand with the four younger siblings as an innocent apprentice? Either way, it would be a challenge.

When it came to things outside of my comfort zone, I'd have, a tendency to go into a shell, listening to everything around me, but not uttering a word. Trying to comprehend how things are structured and why they are arranged in a specific way was, at times, a bit confusing. I felt like the anesthetics of functionality wasn't serving its purpose. My brain wasn't being used to its full potential. However, in order to come out of the shell, I needed to know and understand specific points.

The overcrowded conditions of our living arrangement only added to my difficulties. I, too, shifted out of balance. As a result, I felt crushed and the red flags were up. I, along with my siblings, began to make many complaints and ask several questions:

- *Hey! Is it necessary that we all sleep in the same room?*
- *Do I have a choice to be here?*
- *How can I obey regulations when there are limitations on my freedom?*
- *I do not know if I am accepting or denying this setup.*
- *Where do I put these obligations?*
- *Move over, you are sitting on my tolerance.*
- *What happened to my acceptance?*

No matter what method or approach we choose to use in the process of life, any move we make in reaching our destiny is by way of our own decision. How well we accept and tolerate the order of things will determine our future. Our eternal life with Jesus is not at risk, if we choose the right decision to follow Him. In doing so, this allows our spirit to bring forth its entire memory. This memory includes having a connection with our Heavenly Father.

As Christians, can we hold on to the key of knowledge and absorb all the information intended for our future? Yes, absolutely. During the process of approaching the appreciation phase of any arrangement, there will be setbacks. Is it possible for the same barriers that plagued the little Baby Boomers mentioned earlier to appear causing believers in Christ the same problems? Yes, you bet it can. The enemy of God is everywhere, he can plan an attack on anyone, especially those unexpected.

> *"For the Lord sees clearly what a man does, examining every path he takes. An evil man is held captive by his own sins; they are ropes that catch and hold him. He will die for lack of self-control; he will be lost because of his great foolishness."*
> *(Proverbs 5:21-23, NLT)*

> "To keep me from becoming conceited because of the surpassing greatness of the revelations, a thorn was given me in the flesh, a messenger of Satan to harass me, to keep me from becoming conceited." *(2 Corinthians 12:7, ESV)*

Sin is a transgression against God's sovereignty and we must do our best not to sin against Him. Any act of violation against His Word or His promises is sin. Issues of self-control and fleshly desires will remain challenges for the development of an improved character. For some, these issues remain a struggle. Taking the shifts of the struggle in stride, as the Apostle Paul, and using each opportunity to get into a spiritually submissive position to God will allow us to submit to His entire order of things.

CHAPTER 2

SUBMISSION

"Submit to one another out of reverence for Christ."
(Ephesians 5:21, NIV)

W hen we offer ourselves to the authority of another, we're putting forth an effort to submit. Surrendering to the controlling power on that level is a character act. During this act, one gives up and relinquishes a limited amount of power over self; they are no longer in full command of themselves. Being directly under the controlling influence of another individual and accepting a certain amount of what feels like pressure and force is submission.

To be submissive, one is required to develop and display the qualities of acceptance and tolerance. It's a character development. Advancing our character improves behavior as well; pleasing qualities do not come overnight. This is a process that takes place over time. For some people, this can be a long and drawn-out course. Depending on the required extent of development needed, a pleasing character may take quite some time to develop. Such improvements require patience.

We may wonder:

- How can my character be changed?
- How can my character develop into one that is pleasing to God?
- How can I please my authority figure?
- Who is my authority figure?
- How can I have a pleasant attitude in the face of others?
- How does my character affect those around us?
- What is with my current character and behavior?

Answers to these questions and others as we go further in this book. On one hand, there are some who may not be conscious and aware of the fact that their character is off track and in need of an adjustment. On the other hand, some may have problems along the way in developing their character into being Christ like.

The Apostle Paul (though not one of the twelve original apostles) was one who taught the Gospel of Jesus Christ. Paul tells us, *"We can rejoice, too, when we run into problems and trials, for we know that they help us develop endurance. And endurance develops strength of character, and character strengthens our confident hope of salvations"* (Romans 5:3-5, NLT).

As a six-year-old, I certainly had no knowledge of the words "character" and "behavior," therefore, I had no reason to wonder if character even existed as part of a person. Over fifty years later, I'm still compelled to scream out in a loud voice for the world to hear that I had all along a gift from God. The gift of *grace*. God's grace through Jesus Christ is undeserving, at the same time, made available to all who believe Jesus is Lord. By the presence of God's Holy Spirit, this gift is free and it's what makes the difference in our lives.

Somewhere during the training course, grace came to me in abundance. When it rains, it pours; and when God gives, He pours in abundance. The gift of grace made it possible for me to acquire the knowledge and understanding needed in order to make the right decision and find my correct position. This position is programed in God's will. The gift of grace made it possible for me to maintain sanity in, the midst of chaos, gave me the power to stand against the forces of evil.

Through practice and repeats, the discipline paid off in that the message came through loud and clear. It changed my perception of order and arrangement. Afterwards, I began to observe each matter in a different view. Apart from the fact, I came to realize everything under the sun and moon is of a specific order. Things are arranged a certain way as an explanation and sometimes beyond our understanding.

One may wonder what connection grace has to do with submission. The same little girl who needed help in overcoming the impulses to reject order did not understand either. Sometimes, an intervention from the Spirit of God is the only help that will promote true success in us.

Grace is the intervention that stepped in, connected me to knowledge, and gave me the ability to identify with the meaning of submission.

> Paul says, "*The spirit helps us in our weakness. For we do not know what to pray for as we ought, but the Spirit himself intercedes for us with groanings too deep for words*" (Romans 8:26, ESV).

This gift of grace from God provides the understanding to all of us that a system in place incorporates structure and union. No matter how big, small, plenty, or less the structure may be, the unification is complete when there is an arrangement of specific orders put into place. Grace also enables you and me to get things done to completion, especially those things that are difficult to do, such as submitting.

There are obstacles that may hinder and prevent us from developing into loving human beings. What are these obstacles that inhibits the flow of God's love within us? Anything or anyone that hinders or blocks spiritual progress. For example, we oftentimes set out to gain the quality of submission, with no avail. Many times, we fail in modifying our behavior to complete the mission. The special gift of grace we receive from God soothes the progress, giving us added strength to overcome obstacles while we are in training.

The Apostle Paul faced an obstacle and he requested to have the thorn removed because it was a nagging discomfort for him. Could Paul still submit himself to the Lord in, spite of the thorn? Absolutely! The Lord replied to him, the grace He has given to him is enough, to help overcome that particular problem. With the Lord's help, Paul was able to accomplish the mission that had been assigned to him in spreading the Gospel. Paul's obstacle remaining in place was for his own sake and was a character growth.

> Paul said, "*Even though I have received such wonderful revelations from God. So, to keep me from becoming proud, I was given a thorn in my flesh, a messenger from Satan to torment me and keep me from becoming proud.*" (2 Corinthians 12:7-9)

The good thing is, grace is a gift from God. This same grace produces changes to our behavior and makes the differences in our character. Grace develops, alters, maintains, sustains, modifies, transforms, adjusts, and corrects our character. In, spite of the improvements needed, grace helps while we are on the road of change.

> *"Grace was given to each one of us according to the measure of Christ's gift." (Ephesians 4:7-8, ESV)*

- How can I obtain the gift of grace?
- Do I have to qualify to receive the gift of grace?
- How much or how large will it be?
- Is it a permanent gift?

These questions and more may arise in an attempt to seek spiritual help and guidance. As we continue to search the Scriptures, the Bible gives clear answers to these questions and more. In the meantime, mandatory self-assistance is required on our part. The greatest help we can give ourselves is by practicing goodness toward other people and filling our love bucket and emptying them periodically. Consistent practice in some ways brings about perfection.

In, order for our behavior to continue developing and blossoming into full Christ-like character, our new morals must be in motion. Otherwise, how will we know if our character is changing for the good? By paying attention to our actions and reactions. Take heed when another believer brings something to our attention. Start with the simple things and grow. While practicing along with the grace of God, one acquires the ability to develop their character and display a submissive attitude that is pleasing to God, Jesus Christ, or whomever has earthly authority over us. Here is a list of some of the simple things.

- Be kind to others.
- Display meekness by refusing to complain.
- Have patience with difficult people.
- Show consideration in circumstances that may affect another person's behavior.

- Be humble in any situation that provokes wrath.
- Be nice and show respect to a rude people.
- Display courtesy to disruptive individuals.
- Say "I'm sorry" even when we do not think we are in the wrong.
- Offer, assistance to a weak and fragile person.
- Say thank you during those times when we are not satisfied.
- Stay clear of gaining advantages by way of vulnerable people.

Some may not realize the mysterious power of God can produce amazing results, change any situation, and control any event. As time goes by, we understand orderly things are significant and we realize the reason these arrangements are necessary. By putting good behaviors into practice daily, the power of God that produced the spiritual qualities of our Lord Jesus Christ can produce those same qualities in us. These qualities will emerge from us to be witnessed by others.

The process we use in developing the quality of submission or any other Christ-like behavior requires us to have the fruits of God's spirit present. For example, the quality of "long-suffering" produces tolerance. Tolerance is necessary in cooperating with an order given by another person in authority. Long-suffering teaches patience and it moves us away from the thought of complaining. The fruits of God's spirit are to be embedded within us in order to submit to any arrangement and be submissive under authority.

> *"The fruit of the Spirit is love, joy, peace, patience, kindness, goodness, faithfulness, gentleness, self-control; against such things there is no law." (Galatians 5:22-23, ESV)*

As we submit to God, we are showing Him that we have belief in His will. Because of this belief, we are relinquishing the dominance we have over ourselves. If there is doubt and confusion present within us, submission may be difficult and sometimes impossible to acquire. Our efforts to adhere to His Word never go unnoticed by God.

Yes, the world views an act of submission as a failure or abnormal behavior. Submission is indeed an act displayed through our willingness to be in harmony of a new purpose. As we let go of the control, we have over ourselves, feelings of an undesired flimsiness may arise. Consequently, relying and depending on someone other than self is sometimes difficult to contend with. It can be even harder for some women because there is a greater urge of concern to take care of things. For all of us, letting go of the power to direct our own life is not part of our human nature.

Therefore, an act of submission can easily be misunderstood, misread, and viewed as a disadvantage. Why? Because by nature, we are born preservers. We want to protect that which forms an enclosure around us. Our natural desire as preservers is to safeguard, protect, and defend ourselves from any and everything that restrains us. Sadly, this includes the possibility of shielding ourselves from God, especially if we do not know Him or understand His orderly arrangement of things.

Submissiveness is not a negative trait because God has given all of us command to submit to those in authority over us. God's way has always proven to be perfect for all humans. He gives us this directive in order that we may have the best life possible while on earth.

— CHAPTER 3 —

SPIRITUAL SUBMISSION

Looking at submission from a spiritual point of view is vital to working toward the position of submissiveness. Recognizing and understanding the importance of obedience is a key component. The reference here is the act of submission, which brings glory to God's holy name.

Submission is like having the personality of a sheep and allowing Jesus to shepherd us. Jehovah God wants us to be as sheep that are naturally inclined to follow their leader. Sheep are humble, easily trained and controlled. Sheep usually become stressed when separated from their flock. They are quick to flee in the face of danger and allowed to roam freely only in areas free of predators. While sheep are walking with their shepherd, they are safe from the attack of wolves.

An online article titled, "A Beginners Guide to Raising Sheep" defines the behavior of sheep as "an animal's response to its environment." It goes on to say:

> Sheep are best known for their strong flocking (herding) and following instinct. When one sheep moves, the rest will follow, even when it's not a good idea. They will run from what frightens them and band together in large groups for protection. This is the only protection they have from predators. It is harder for a predator to pick a sheep out of a group than to go after a few strays.
>
> Changes in normal behavior can be an early sign of illness in sheep. Not much difference when it comes to humans. The most obvious example of illness relates

to the sheep's most natural behavioral, their flocking instinct. A sheep or lamb that is isolated from the rest of the flock is likely showing early signs of illness (unless it is lost). Even the last sheep through the gate should be suspected of not feeling well, especially if it is usually one of the first. (*Sheep 201, A Beginners Guide to Raising Sheep*)

Having a submissive behavior toward God shows we are like sheep. It also shows we have received the Word of God and agree with His method of arrangements. Our submission to God is submitting to biblical authority, different from submitting to human authority. Our Heavenly Father must never be placed on the same level with humans. He is sovereign and above all things He has made; whether it is humans, angels, or spirits; God is superior. Our submission to God overrules our submission to earthly rulers, no matter who they are.

> *"With my whole heart, I seek you; let me not wander from your commandments! I have stored up your word in my heart, that I might not sin against you." (Psalm 119:10-11, ESV)*

King Jehoshaphat was a king of Judah who reigned for twenty-five years; he knew the power of God and His sovereignty. He prayed often and was wise to trust in God.

> *"Jehoshaphat stood in the middle of the assembly of Judah and Jerusalem, in the house of the Lord, before the new court, and said, "O Lord, God of our fathers, are you not God in heaven? You rule over all the kingdoms of the nations. In your hand are power and might, so that none is able to withstand you."" (2 Chronicles 20:5-6 ESV)*

Let's always be prayerful and wise, trust in God the way Jehoshaphat did. Let's trust in the Lord and give Him the ultimate glory He deserves. Acquiring the act of submission to God shows that we are submitting to

His way of doing things. This trust must be manifested especially during those times of difficulty and when we don't fully understand instructions given through authority. This is the perfect moment to push forward and reach for understanding. At the same time, exercising kindness and goodness toward other people during these moments gives us a boost.

The urge to resist may arise and we may have, a tendency to rebel against God's authority, but we must keep trusting and praying. When this urge creeps upon us, what should we do? We must pray and ask for God's help in dealing with the situation. Always pay close attention to the teachings of Jesus outlined in the Bible; trust in Him. Jesus repeatedly mentions to us in the Bible to pray and search the Scriptures that are outlined in order to be equipped with knowledge.

This knowledge Jesus talks about is spiritual wisdom, and it is powerful. Let us make the effort to find out God's will and advice for our everyday life, including our circumstances and situations. Using the Bible's guidelines, we find different ways to maintain stability and remain on the road to spiritual success. It takes effort and commitment to gain the spiritual knowledge intended for us to succeed.

> Jesus says to us, "*My message is not my own; it comes from God who sent me. Anyone who wants to do the will of God will know whether my teaching is from God or is merely my own*" (John 7:16-17, NLT).

> The Apostle Paul lifted up prayers on our behalf: "*I have not stopped thanking God for you. I pray for you constantly, asking God, the glorious Father of our Lord Jesus Christ to give you spiritual wisdom and insight so that you might grow in your knowledge of God*" (Ephesians 1:16-18, NLT).

As we take a deeper look into biblical submission, let's be confident and push forward for an understanding of God's Word. Being in a frame of mind that allows us to focus solely on God places us in the correct position, so we can submit to Him. Yes, there are times when we may be limited in our energy needed to push onward.

Trying to put forth the extra effort can be a struggle for some because the self-confidence of that person is constantly at war with the desire to submit. Part of this self-confidence is thinking, *If I let go of the control I have over myself, I will undoubtedly fall.* But, you won't—only if you trust in God.

In, spite of distress one may be feeling, prayer and a consistent behavior of obedience to God's Word during this practice aids in getting past the obstructive issues.

> *"In my distress, I called upon the Lord; to my God I cried for help. From his temple, he heard my voice, and my cry to him reached his ears." (Psalm 18:6, ESV)*

The Prophet Jeremiah was called by the Lord to give prophetic word to the nation of Israel because of their disobedience to Jehovah God.

> *"But this command I give to them; Obey my voice, and I will be your God, and you shall be my people. And walk in all the way that I command you, that it may be well with you." (Jeremiah 7:23, ESV)*

Failure to submit to God may also be due to self-importance of pride and arrogance. These two are other contributing factors to rebellion. While in the process of submitting, some may even feel as though the potential liberty given to each human at birth may be gone. The idea of being individually free on earth without restraints can be somewhat soothing. This alone may create a major struggle in our effort to submit to order. Therefore, the natural response of humans is to resist in order to defend what we know as independence.

Unfortunately, this rebellion is an act against God's order. Being obedient to His Word will overrule the urges to be repugnant. Gaining spiritual knowledge through the Word of God and knowing what He says concerning submission is crucial to the development of our character. This knowledge prevents us from having doubts and rebelling against authority. Searching the Scriptures gives satisfactory answers to these questions and more—it gives proof to doubt and encourages obedience.

The Apostle Paul's letter to the Romans is of use for us, too. In his letter in part he writes, *"Everyone must submit to governing authorities. For all authority comes from God, and those in positions of authority have been place there by God. So, anyone who rebels against authority is rebelling against what God has instituted, and they will be punished"* (Romans 13:1-2, NLT).

IMPORTANT THINGS TO REMEMBER:

Who is the originator of spiritual things? The Bible tells us that God, our Heavenly Father, is the sole creator of spiritual order. He has always known that confusion may escalate, and His awareness is certain that things may sometimes be foggy to us. He gave us His spiritual order to help with our weak morals as we continue to decline farther away from Him. Understanding our Heavenly Father and His way of doing things goes far beyond our observation.

> Proverbs 30:4 (NLT) says, *"Who but God goes up to heaven and comes back down? Who holds the wind in his fist? Who wraps up the oceans in his cloak? Who has created the whole wide world? What is his name-and his son's name? Tell me if you know!"*

What is the value of spiritual order? There are no perfect people in this world. Some are selfish, inconsiderate, or just plain confused. The value of spiritual order is doing things God's way. It is vital in that it promotes peace and harmony among all. The priesthood of the Levites and the priesthood of Christ were setup to train God's people. Under these settings that God established, people would obtain stability and a higher level of morality.

The Bible gives us an account of the Levites who, at God's order, were chosen to the priesthood (Numbers 3:5-10, 4:46-49, ESV). We then read in Hebrews that today, Jesus Christ is our High Priest.

> *"So then, since we have a great High Priest who has entered heaven, Jesus the Son of God, let us hold firmly to what we believe." (Hebrews 4:14, NLT)*

Is there a command to submit? Imperfection will always remain as a part of human nature. When rebellion shows, that means a wrong turn has been taken somewhere along the path. As a result, instructions given by God through direct control and contact are available to steer and guide this person back on track. Paul gives strong advice on the importance of having a submissive attitude. The advice he gives is to all those who are faithfully serving the Lord including leaders, husbands, wives, children, servants, and more.

A word given to the prophet, Jeremiah for Israel was by God himself. These words serve as a benefit and protects our life in the same manner. In, order for the Lord Almighty to be your God, repentance should be a normal response and obedience to every word is our lifeline. Obedience is submission.

> *This is what the Lord Almighty, the God of Israel says: "For when I brought your ancestors out of Egypt and spoke to them, I did not just give them commands about burnt offerings and sacrifices, but I gave them this command: Obey me, and I will be your God and you will be my people." (Jeremiah 7:21-23 NIV)*

See also Ephesians 5:1-33 (ESV).

What are the benefits of submission? There is great reward for all those who align themselves with the order of things. A spiritual connection is formed, giving one the advantage of reaping a higher perceptive. Submission to God benefits every man, woman, and child.

If you look around, can you see the works of the Lord in the lives of other faithful followers who are serving and worshiping Him? Can other people see the Lord's work in your life? Like the Prophet Isaiah, do you recognize His power when you are in His presence? (see Isaiah Chapter 6, ESV)

The main goal of our Christian life is to declare the glory of God and bring honor to Him. The glory of God is expressed in the Bible as His holy presence and power. Our submission to God brings Him glory.

Jesus said, *"In the same way, let your good deeds shine out for all to see, so that everyone will praise your heavenly Father"* (Matthew 5:16, NLT).

> *"The heavens declare the glory of God, and the sky above proclaims his handiwork." (Psalm 19:1)*

Peter, an Apostle of Jesus, says:

> *"Be subject for the Lord's sake to every human institution, whether it be to the emperor as supreme, or to governors as sent by Him to punish those who do evil and to praise those who do good. For this is the will of God, that by doing good you should put to silence the ignorance of foolish people." (1 Peter 2:13-15 ESV)*

CHAPTER 4

SACRED HARMONY

*"But I want you to understand that the head of every man
is Christ, the head of a wife is her husband, and the head of
Christ is God." (1 Corinthians 11:3, ESV)*

The spiritual order of submission is God's method of arrangement. This authoritative direction would bring about the Glory of God. We have a chance to be included in this glorious systematic arrangement. Let's always remember our Heavenly Father is superior, therefore He is the supreme ruler in the force of His spiritual order.

God has arranged His kingdom with order, in a manner that brings admiration to His holy name. This is a kingdom that will never fall. Apart from these facts, this arrangement releases benefits to those who align themselves under the control and authority of Him. Jehovah God's spiritual order is in effect.

* **Jehovah God, Heavenly Father**
* **Jesus Christ, Son of God**
* **Spiritual Leaders**
* **Man / Husband**
* **Woman / Wife**
* **Children**

According to the Bible, this is the proper order of the arrangement set by God. The Apostle Paul elaborated on the subject of spiritual order in his letter written to the church at Corinth in 1 Corinthians 11. He also wrote a letter to the Colossians. He knew the challenges they faced, and he wanted to correct the serious problems in these churches. Paul provided them with godly counsel in order that their conducts would be pleasing to God.

> In Paul's encouraging letter to the Colossians he wrote, *"So, you also are complete through your union with Christ, who is the head over every ruler and authority"* (Colossians 2:10, NLT).

Under God's rule, some have a different role to play, sometimes more than one role. Their responsibilities vary, and the degree of control is limited. To rule is to have controlling power over one or more than one person. The controlling power is for the purpose of organizing difficult conditions and managing environments. To rule also means to exercise authority and control over situations and circumstances. Rulers give orders, make major decisions in a matter, and lay down specific regulations.

Jesus Christ is directly placed in position of authority by God and given the capacity to control His Father's kingdom. It is safe to say He observes all of us under what I call the "Standard of Comparison," which is a distinctive measurement used by the one overseeing and evaluating a person's character.

To elevate His followers to higher standards, Jesus uses the morals He received from God by way of the Holy Spirit and from the written Word of God, the Holy Bible. These requirements are set by God to expose sin in the world and sometimes through individual sin.

> The Prophet Isaiah refers to Jesus as God's chosen one. *"Behold my servant, whom I uphold, my chosen, in whom my soul delights; I have put my Spirit upon him; he will bring forth justice to the nations"* (Isaiah 42:1, NTL).

> One of the twelve apostles, Matthew, writes, *"After his baptism, as Jesus came up out of the water, the heavens were opened and he saw the Spirit of God descending like a dove and settling on him. And a voice from heaven said, 'This is*

my dearly loved Son, who brings me great joy'" (Matthew
3:16-17, NLT).

In His expressions of wisdom, Jesus mentions His obligations to us
by saying He is sent to preach the kingdom of God. He came to earth to
reach those who are oppressed by the enemy, Satan, and those enslaved
by their own sin and evil. The Bible teaches there is no other way to
our Heavenly Father, except by way of Jesus Christ. By accepting Jesus
as our Lord and Savior, we have the opportunity to have everlasting life.
Jesus is the only way we can have a relationship with God. He is the only
source of eternal life in Heaven.

> According to the apostle Luke, Jesus said, *"The Spirit
> of the Lord is upon me, because he has anointed me to
> proclaim good news to the poor. He has sent me to proclaim
> liberty to the captives and recovering of sight to the blind, to
> set at liberty those who are oppressed, to proclaim the year
> of the Lord's favor"* (Luke 4:18-19, ESV).

In music, performance and theory have specific rules of harmony.
These rules are used in gaining the beauty and simplicity of audio for
the listener. This harmony is manipulated using chords, which are a
combination of pitch classes. Most of the harmony comes from two or
more notes sounding simultaneously. It differentiates between various
sounds. These works create a sense of harmony by using chords and
implied bass lines. The implied bass lines are created with low notes of
short duration that many listeners perceive as being the bass note of a
chord.

A German composer and pianist born in 1770 was Ludwig van
Beethoven, one of the most famous influential composers of all time.
He was well known for harmonizing his work. He displayed his musical
talents at an early age and was taught by his father, Johann van Beethoven
and by composer and conductor Christian Neefe. By the age of twenty-
one, he moved to Vienna, where he continued studying composition
and gained a reputation as a virtuoso pianist. In 1798, Beethoven is
reported to have suffered a fit induced by a rage at the interruption of his

work. After falling over, he got up to find himself deaf. He had suffered hearing loss.

He went on to conduct music and perform publicly until the year 1811. Many of his most admired works come from the last fifteen years of his life, which included the compositions Fur Elise, Symphony No. 5, and Ode to Joy. In 1827, after being bedridden most of his remaining months, Beethoven died on March 26 during a thunderstorm. It must have been music to his ears.

Most folks happily consume music that is pleasing to their ears. Can you imagine going to a theater with the expectations of listening to some good music, but instead of it being pleasing to your ears, the opening chords sounding as wicked as several drawers of utensils falling from way above the floor? Harmony wasn't invited to this theater. What excruciating pain. Nerve hairs in your inner ear began to shiver. You say to yourself, "This is horrible." It's so ghastly you want to get up and walk out of the theater without finding out whether the next set of chords is worth listening.

What makes beautiful music? It's instrumental and vocal acoustics that provide our ears and brain with a gratifying environment. It brings joy to some and motivation to others. It's incredible to think that vibrations unseen by the human eye can bring on an emotional experience and a state of wellbeing. Beautiful music is the sweet, pleasing, and harmonious sound waves that give the listener something to smile about.

Listening to beautiful music is that which was directed under Beethoven. Beautiful music is like the sound the Lord describes to Job, a man who was blameless and upright. The Lord challenges Him to answer a question. The Lord asked him in Job 38:4-7, "Where were you .... while the morning stars sang together and all the angels shouted for joy."

Similar to music, in order for any ruler to lead effectively, the rules of harmony must apply in ordinary life. Those under authority must be in harmony and in their proper place of submission. A system of measuring progress is assigned to each ruler in authority. The ruler uses the "Standard of Comparison" to check actions and behaviors of the ones under their authority. Without an established system, there is no submission, which means there is no order.

The ruler then presents these principles to his or her subordinates in the form of writings, demonstrations, and explanations. Using these different techniques helps the dependent ones to understand mandate and instructions. In addition, a healthy lifestyle of the ruler will support the progress of the inferior ones. The ones under care rely on a stabilized environment to keep the pace.

> *"Words alone will not discipline a servant; the words may be understood, but they are not heeded." (Proverbs 29:19, NLT)*

> Paul's advice to leaders: *"If God has given you leadership ability, take the responsibility seriously. And if you have a gift of showing kindness to others, do it gladly" (Romans 12:7b, NLT).*

The person in authority recognizes the excellence of those under them by comparing their improvements. By observing the behaviors that may be declining morally, the leader is able to locate and validate each person's value and worth. Leaders provide the assistance to that person in order to make the necessary adjustments needed for growth. The progression of each individual character is cheered, along with hopes for a greater good. Order and stability are born into this person's life.

In the book of Matthew, the apostle gives an account of things Jesus did to enlighten the people's knowledge of God. Matthew mentions (through the power of the Holy Spirit) that Jesus performed several miracles: healing of the sick and driving demons out of people. Jesus understood the realms of evil and the clever tricks of Satan. Many people saw the benefits of Jesus casting out demons and performing other miracles. These same people became interested in submitting themselves to God.

> *"Jesus went throughout Galilee, teaching in their synagogues, proclaiming the good news of the kingdom, and healing every disease and sickness among the people. News about him spread all over Syria." (Matthew 4:23-24a, NIV)*

The position of all those in authority provides support to ones easily swayed into destruction. Such ones in authoritative positions are pastors, ministers, bishops, deacons, judges, teachers, husbands, wives, mothers, and many others. Every Christian leader must do their best to protect those under their care. If you are in an authoritative role, do you have compassion for those under you? Are you, observant of the preventive care needed for their spiritual wellbeing? Shepherds' care and guidance are needed because some, like sheep, have a wandering nature.

> Jesus gave Simon Peter an assignment of authority to take care of His sheep. He said, *"Simon son of John, do you love me?' 'Yes, Lord,' Peter said, 'You know I love you.' 'Then take care of my sheep,' Jesus said"* (John 21:16, NLT).

If one has an assignment to rule in God's kingdom, does this mean his or her conduct may be exempt from the same regulations Jesus gave Simon Peter? Not at all. The same regulations apply to all leaders in authority. If one has not been assigned to lead, does this mean he or she may be excused from compelling others to remember regulations? No.

It does not matter who we are or how long we have been on earth; each one of us has an obligation to submit to divine order. This order is so that everyone has an opportunity to enter the gates of Heaven. We are all accountable in one form or another for each other. The righteousness of God is to be upheld always. God is true, and He never changes. He is always there with His arms wide open, waiting for those who are lost to sin.

Paul addresses unfaithfulness to God. *"What if some were unfaithful? Does their faithlessness mollify the faithfulness of God? By no means! Let God be true though everyone were a liar, as it is written; That you may be justified in your words, and prevail when you are judged"* (Romans 3:3-4, ESV).

THE FALL OF A CORPORATION

Giovanni de Medici enjoyed the reputation of a kindly man. He was honest, understanding, and humane. No one could mistake the worldly wise, shrewdness in his hooded eyes, nor the determined set of his large chin. He was never eloquent, but in his talk, there were occasional flashes of wit, rendered all the more disarming by the habitually lugubrious expression of his face.

The Medici Bank was a financial institution in Italy created by the Medici family during the fifteenth century (1397–1494). It was the most important financial institution in Europe. The largest and most respected bank in Europe during its prime, Medici Bank was at the top of its rank. Its super-elevation made it the chief bank for the Roman Catholic curia, and it had branches in the major cities of Italy, as well as in London, Lyon, Geneva, Bruges, and Avignon.

The first in his family to enter into the banking business on his own, Giovanni de Medici was the founder of Medici Bank. He became influential in the Florentine government. Members of the Medici family became involved in banking in the city of Florentine in the later 1300s. There were some estimates that the Medici family was, for a period of time, the wealthiest family in Europe. With this monetary wealth, the family acquired political power initially in Florence, Italy and later in the wider spheres of Italy and Europe. Several Medici Banks were opened and flourished in many regions.

After Giovanni's death in 1429 his son, Cosimo the Elder, took control of the bank. In 1434, this son of Giovanni became gran maestro and the Medici became the unofficial head of state of the Florentine republic. By 1494, some of its branches ceased to exist. The central Florentine branch was burned by the mob, the Lyons branch was taken over by a rival firm, and the Roman branch struck off on its own, despite the branch being bankrupt in general.

After flourishing for over a century, this organization was on the verge of crumbling. The branches that did not die off on their own generally met their end with the collapse of the Medici's political power in Florence in 1494. Savonarola and the Pope had struck out against them.

Ironically, they would suffer still more debt when a cardinal became Pope Leo X and inquired after the 11,243 gold florins, he had deposited with the branch back when he was with the Medici bank. Even at the time of its downfall, the Medici Bank was the biggest bank in Europe, with at least seven branches over fifty factors. This corporation built by the Medici family suffered a great loss; their kingdom had fallen.

Jesus is king of the kingdom set up by Jehovah God. This is a kingdom that will never fall because it cannot be shaken by worldly events. Jesus has the power to do far better than any earthly ruler. He is faithful and obedient to God. He has experienced the things that are sacred and holy. His knowledge of heavenly things surpasses the understanding of ordinary man.

Christ is perfectly holy and without flaws. He knows the exact spiritual order of things and why God has arranged them in a way of glorifying Himself. This arrangement set up by God is perfect and we are privileged to take part in His kingdom.

> *"And the Spirit of the Lord shall rest upon him, the Spirit of Wisdom and understanding, the Spirit of counsel and might, the Spirit of knowledge and the fear of the Lord."* (Isaiah 11:2, ESV)

> Daniel interprets a dream for King Nebuchadnezzar, in part saying, *"And in the days of those kings the God of heaven will set up a kingdom that shall never be destroyed, nor shall the kingdom be left to another people. It shall break to pieces all these kingdoms and bring them to an end, and it shall stand forever"* (Daniel 2:44, ESV).

CHAPTER 5

BENEFITS OF OBEDIENCE

Being in a submissive position is beneficial to all parties involved. It brings honor and glory to the name of Jehovah God, the creator of Heaven and Earth. There is safety and protection of obedience for all those under authority. There is also reward for all those in position of leadership over another.

The Holocaust is one of the most traumatic episodes of modern history. It has also yielded some astounding stories of bravery, faith, and obedience. The Holocaust was a genocide in which Adolf Hitler's Nazi Germany and its collaborators killed about six million Jews in the deadliest systematic extermination in history. From 1941 to 1945, Jews suffered persecution at the hands of Adolf Hitler. He aimed to eliminate Jews from Germany, whom he considered unworthy of life.

The persecution and genocide were carried out in stages, culminating in what Nazis termed the "Final Solution to the Jewish Question." This was an agenda to exterminate Jews in Europe. Initially the German government passed laws to exclude Jews from civil society, most prominently the Nuremberg Laws of 1935.

Nazis established a network of concentration camps starting in 1933 and ghettos following the outbreak of World War II in 1939. The Jews would either go to the ghettos, a section of a city populated by a certain ethnic group or go into hiding. By the end of 1942, victims were regularly transported by freight trains to extermination camps where, if they survived the journey, most were systematically killed in gas chambers.

Those who had been selected to die were led to gas chambers and within minutes, they were dead. This continued until the end of World War II in Europe.

In France, a Jewish family was hidden by some French nationals in the basement of their house. The Jewish family waited and waited for their deliverance. While waiting, they remained faithful and obedient to the God of Israel, Jehovah. In facing death, they did not relinquish their faith in God. At the end of the war, the following words were found scribbled on the wall of that basement:

> "I believe in the sun even when it does not shine.
> I believe in love even when it is not given.
> I believe in God even when he is silent."

During his trip to Poland in 2006, Pope Benedict XVI (Joseph Ratzinger) stood in the Auschwitz-Birkenau death camp and asked, "Where was God in those days? Why was he silent? How could he permit this endless slaughter, this triumph of evil?" The Pope blamed the deaths of the Jews on Hitler, the criminals, and those who followed Hitler.

The Pope also acknowledged the reality of Jew-hatred that was driven by hostility, not just toward Jews, but others as well. He also acknowledged the hatred toward the message of God-based ethics the Jews first brought to the world. The Pope said, "Deep down, those vicious criminals wanted to kill the God who called Abraham, who spoke on Sinai and laid down principles to serve as a guide for mankind, principles that are eternally valid." He understood that hatred is destroying the world.

James, one of the twelve apostles of Jesus Christ, tells you and I that there is safety involved when submitting ourselves to God. This does not mean the Jews that were murdered during the Holocaust didn't submit themselves to God. There are times when bad things happen to good people. Ultimately, we don't know the reasons for what God allows and disallows to happen here on Earth.

There are times when innocent lives are lost at the hands of evil. The world is filled with sinful people. There is evil in every country, and there is no way we can possibly fathom why this happened to the Jews who were in Germany and Eastern Europe at that time. What we do know is God's love for His people never changes.

> *"Submit yourselves therefore to God. Resist the devil and he will flee from you." (James 4:7, KJV)*

What we do know is God loves us unconditionally and His love endures forever. The Israelites suffered persecution in Egypt at the hands of Pharaoh, but at the end of the day, God extended His loving care to His people upon their entrance into the Promised Land.

> *"So, Joshua ordered the officers of the people: 'Go through the camp and tell the people, Get your provisions ready. Three days from now you will cross the Jordan here to go in and take possession of the land the Lord your God is giving you for your own.'" (Joshua 1:10-11, NIV)*

However, we must still obey Him even when life hurts. We all go through difficult times in life and sometimes things don't look promising. Yet, we must believe God when He says he will send an angel to prepare the way for us. Trust Him even when the sun is not shining. Believe in God even when He is silent. At the end of the day, there is safety in obedience.

> *"If you listen carefully to what he (the angel) says and do all that I say, I will be an enemy to your enemies and will oppose those who oppose you." (Exodus 23:22, NIV)*

While we're listening, and adhering to the message from the Lord, we are safe from the snares and traps of the devil. When we submit to God, we are directly under His authority. His power protects us from Satan and he will flee from us when we accept Jesus as our Lord and Savior. Satan is a spirit and he controls the realm of evil. He is in the midst of every chaotic situation. When we submit to God, the devil will run away from us because we are proving to him that we refuse evil. We will not go along with his scheme.

Being sheltered under the Lord, we have a sense of spiritual relaxation; we are at ease knowing we are safe. During this relaxation, we are still resisting the devil because we are not responding to his tactics. Being under the controlling power of Almighty God, we are automatically protected. This shield of protection keeps us from harm and danger of the evil one.

> *"Fear of the Lord leads to life, bringing security and protection from harm." (Proverbs 19:23, NLT)*

Peter gives counsel on respecting fellow Christians who are in authority. He tells us that to offer ourselves to God is to obey every ordinance of man and do this for the sake of the Lord. We are to accept every law that man has placed in effect before us. Accepting these values, we enhance the work that Jesus Christ did while on earth. The law of man safeguards and protects each, individual from hurt or possibly damaging another, which is what Jesus tries to instill in everyone.

> *"Be subject for the Lord's sake to every human institution, whether it be to the emperor as supreme, or to governors as sent by him to punish those who do evil and to praise those who do good. For this is the will of God, that by doing good you should put to silence the ignorance of foolish people."* (1 Peter 2:13-15, ESV)

In the United States, the law of the land is constructed by man through the federal and state government. There is coordination between these officials and their functioning parts are harmonious. They share power in countless ways: collecting taxes, building roads, establishing courts, and making and enforcing laws, to name a few. If we pay close attention to these laws, we will recognize that a majority of the ordinances produced are from several sections of the Holy Bible.

Those in control of the land ordinances in the United States are presidents, governors, mayors, judges, police officers, and military officers. These are the ones that keep our country stabilized and ensure healthy communities. Good leadership is crucial for high morale and building personalities. The world is a better place when there is quality leadership.

Having and showing respect for these officials is not just an ordinance from man; it is also a direct ordinance from God as well. When we are obedient to the law of man, there is an advantage to the kingdom of God. He receives the glory from the obedience of civilization.

> *"Let every person be subject to the governing authorities. For there is no authority except from God, and those that exist have been instituted by God. Therefore, whoever resists the authorities resists what God has appointed, and those who resist will incur judgment." (Romans 13:1-2, ESV)*

Subjecting ourselves to these laws is an advantage to God's kingdom. It's an improvement in that the law deals with murderers, hatred, cruelty, greed, evildoers, and wrongdoers. These lawbreakers are apprehended while in their wrongness, reprimanded for their offensive behavior, and then taught to respect others through rehabilitation. This is part of God's will anyway. As an outcome, we may say the ordinance of man is helping in the progress of the kingdom's work.

> *"Obey your leaders and submit to them, for they are keeping watch over your souls, as those who have to give an account. Let them do this with joy and not with groaning, for that would be of no advantage to you." (Hebrews 13:17, ESV)*

We have instructions from God to obey all the ones that have control over us. This means we all have a duty to accept and comply with authority. Here are examples of those in authority and some of the benefits provided. Not necessarily in this order:

- Jesus Christ: Son of God, gave the world the greatest example of a perfect life on earth, died a sinner's death for all to be reunited with His Heavenly Father.
- Pastors and spiritual leaders: shepherds the congregation and leads in their spiritual growth.

- Husbands: Gives love and honor to their wives, provides for and protects his family.
- Wives: Far more precious than jewels. She looks well to the ways of her household. (See Proverbs 31.)
- Parents: Direct children onto the path of righteousness. When they are older, they will not leave it. (See Proverbs 22:6.)
- Deacon: an overseer, takes good care of God's church and his own household. (See 1 Timothy 3.)
- Government: Establishes justice in a country, insure domestic tranquility, promote the general welfare, provide for the common defense, and secure the blessings of liberty. (See: The Constitutions of The United States of America.)
- Teachers: Inspire and encourage students to see the best in themselves.

There are several benefits of leadership. The benefits of having leaders among us is they guard every part of our human nature and protect the spiritual, emotional, and physical part of our being. The rulers give an account for the souls on which they keep an eye. They have, to give an account to their authority figure. The leaders provide a report and explanation to a higher authority of whoever placed them in charge. The whole purpose of the ruler is to influence the weak to make progress and improve.

There are many benefits to having and obeying leaders. Another reason to cooperate is those under authority will benefit from having a leader. Ones in charge are interested in giving a good report. The leaders do not want to be in an awkward position by having to give an embarrassing report on an individual.

A bad report is grief to those in charge because it shines a negative light on the leaders. In some cases, it may show that the ruler is not handling their position of authority well. At the same time, a grievous report is a disadvantage to the individuals under authority because certain ones may not be gaining from the order of the arrangement. After all, there are great blessings for all those involved.

In my home study room, there's a shoeshine brush that has been sitting on the bookshelf for years. It's made of authentic wood and 100%

horsehair. Once in a while, I pick it up and am reminded of my service to the kingdom of God. This brush also reminds me of Jesus' words told to His disciples in Matthew 20:28, *"Just as the Son of Man did not come to be served, but to serve, and to give his life as a ransom for many."*

Dan Cathy, an American businessman, is chairman, president, and CEO of Chick-fil-A. The chain was founded by his late father, S. Truett Cathy. In January 2009, Dan came as guest speaker of our church, First Baptist of West Monroe, Louisiana. He talked about how his father's legacy of helping others lives on in him. One evening, while visiting, he gave a lecture in the Fellowship Hall called "Leadership Development Tools." He handed out shoeshine brushes to everyone around the room. He then began to inspire us by using the brush to demonstrate how a shoe shiner takes this small instrument to serve others.

He came over to the table where I was seated and asked me to stand. I was nervous because the room was filled with many churchgoers and I had no idea why I was being asked to stand. Dan proceeded to use the smile on my face as an example of the potential employees they hire at Chick-fil-A. This was the same smile I always try to keep on my face. He explained how a genuine smile could go a long way in serving others. A smile can be a blessing to someone else. It can turn a lousy day someone is having into a day of refresh. Try it; you'll be amazed at the results.

— CHAPTER 6 —

THE SPIRIT OF PEACE

"What kind of peace do we seek? Not a Pax Americana enforced on the world by American weapons of war. Not the peace of the grave or the security of the slave. I am talking about genuine peace, the kind of peace that makes life on earth worth living. The kind of peace that enables men and nations to grow and hope to build a better life for their children... not merely peace in our time but peace for all time." (A Strategy of Peace, President John F. Kennedy)

John Fitzgerald "Jack" Kennedy (JFK) was an American politician who served as the thirty-fifth President of the United States from January 1961 until his assassination in November 1963. He met his wife, Jacqueline Lee "Jackie" Bouvier when he was a congressman. A journalist introduced the pair at a dinner party and they became inseparable.

John and Jackie were married one year after he was elected senator, on September 12, 1953. The Kennedy family was one of the most established political families in the United States, having produced a president, three senators, and multiple other representatives, both on the federal and state level. The President was riding in a motorcade, an open car, in downtown Dallas, Texas when the assassin started shooting. With his wife riding next to him, President Kennedy was shot in the head and last his words on earth were, "God, I've been hit."

Today, over fifty years later, his 1963 peace speech titled, "A Strategy of Peace" still inspires us. Kennedy outlined a plan for world peace and it is remembered as one of his finest and most important speeches of all time. It reminds us of how much the world has changed since Moses began recording man's association with God. It also reminds us of just how far we have drifted away from our Heavenly Father.

As children of God, we are given clear instruction on finding peace and following it. Keeping away from evil should be of highest priority when pursuing a state of tranquility for our life. We are to abstain from all appearances of evil and hold fast to that which is good. Keep the tongue and lips from speaking guile. Those things that cause uproar and disturbances among people, stay away.

The Bible tells us that peace is the presence of Christ. Where there is peace, there is also Christ. Peace is also a spirit, one of the excellent qualities of God's nature. Peace has a close association with submission. They are closely related in that freedom of the mind must exist, in order to remain in a submissive position to the one in authority.

Peace was designed by God as a comfort system for us. It also makes sure we are always comfortable. It safeguards the physical, mental, and spiritual part of our being. The spirit of peace helps us to remain in our correct position, which is being submissive to God's will.

The spirit of peace is created and ruled by God, governed by God, and directly under God's leadership. The presence of the spirit of peace has specific benefits. When we have harmony in our lives, it is a blessing from God. Paul mentions one of the Fruit of God's Spirit is peace. This fruit is an excellent quality of God's character. His nature is displayed through the Fruit of the Spirit.

> *"The fruit of the Spirit is love, joy, peace, patience, kindness, goodness, faithfulness, gentleness, self-control; against such things there is no law."* (Galatians 5:22-23, ESV)

> *"May the Lord give strength to his people! May the Lord bless his people with peace!"* (Psalm 29:11 ESV)

In holding fast to a freedom of strife, let's always be aware of thoughts and behaviors that may not be pleasing to God. Stick to words and actions that are decent and becoming of a Christian. This command is given because we are, at times, vulnerable to the sneaky attacks of Satan. He will use something as small as a person's rude behavior to disrupt our peaceful environment. Don't let him do it; always remain humble and in peace.

> *"Keep your tongue from speaking evil and your lips from telling lies! Turn away from evil and do good. Search for peace, and work to maintain it." (Psalm 34:13-14, NLT)*

God is pleased when we voluntarily keep away from evil. He does not force us to righteousness, but it makes him happy when we take a stand against evil. Heaven is especially pleased when we don't take for granted that the angels will rescue us from the midst of evil. We should never purposefully walk in evil and expect other people to risk their spirituality in helping us. This means we must make the wise decision of not becoming entangled with evil.

PURSUING PEACE

How do we keep away from the evils of Satan when it is all around us? To keep away from evil is by having an understanding that evil can conquer a human being. As we read the Word of God, have trust in It, and follow His outlined instructions to stand against evil. The truth gives the ability to organize our lives, and the knowledge gives the necessary skills to stabilize it.

> "The best weapon is to sit down and talk." (Nelson Mandela)

> "I am fundamentally an optimist. Whether that comes from nature or nurture, I cannot say. Part of being optimistic is keeping one's head pointed toward the sun, one's feet moving forward. There were many dark moments when my faith in humanity was sorely tested, but I would not and could not give myself up to despair. That way lays defeat and death." (Nelson Mandela)

Nelson Rolihlahla Mandela became the first black president of South Africa in 1994. He quoted these words in his book titled, *Long Walk to Freedom*. His dedication to fight racial oppression won him the Nobel Peace Prize in 1993 and the presidency of his country. He achieved international recognition for his leadership in rebuilding South Africa's once segregated society. We can compare his leadership to that of Moses in that it was liberation to all those oppressed and his commitments will be cherished throughout history for many years.

We also have the words of King Solomon, inspired by our Heavenly Father. During Solomon's reign over Israel, the Israelites remained under peaceful conditions for forty years. His advice to Israel was to stay away from evil. He describes a form of evil that is sometimes used: the tongue. Solomon warned Israel against this form of evil.

> *"The tongue of the wise commends knowledge, but the mouths of fools pour out folly." (Proverbs 15:2, ESV)*

> *"Death and life are in the power of the tongue, and those who love it will eat its fruits." (Proverbs 18:21, ESV)*

Controlling our tongue is one of the regulations we should all adhere to while traveling the road pursuing the spirit of peace. If we have nothing good to say about another person, let's control our tongue and say nothing. Let's not put our mouth on people in slander because you never know who they are to God. However, this does not mean Christians should compromise their faith and values for the sake of getting along with or pleasing others. Values remain even while in awkward situations.

> *"Do not say, 'I will pay you back for this wrong!' Wait for the Lord, and he will avenge you." (Proverbs 20:22, NIV)*

When peace is present, conditions are usually calm, orderly, and harmonious. The mind, body, and spirit are free of Satan's control. There is a state of quietness with little to no disturbances from Satan or his evil spirits. For example, when peaceful conditions are with the physical body, there is no excessive stimulation. At this point, the body is not easily excited. This activity of the physical body shows a comparison to the mental and spiritual condition of that person.

Usually, disturbances to the body's composure cause it to change or shift out of gear. The same goes for our mental and spiritual composure. Depending on the severity of interference, some changes may be drastic. As a result, if left unnoticed, the individual becomes hooked into a lifestyle that is not pleasing to God.

A PLACE TO LODGE AND REST

Upon locating peace, we can relax and be confident in staying. How can we relax? By knowing and believing we have two great spiritual leaders chosen by God to be, in charge of this lodge. The Bible mentions them by name: Jesus Christ, the Prince of Peace, and Melchizedek, the King of Peace. They are chosen by God as the highest leaders of this resting place. Melchizedek was a man dedicated to conducting peaceful environments and maintaining harmony among all men. Jesus Christ came to earth after Melchizedek and prepared us for the order of peace.

> *"For to us a child is born, to us a son is given; and the government shall be upon his shoulder, and his name shall be called Wonderful Counselor, Mighty God, Everlasting Father, Prince of Peace." (Isaiah 9:6, ESV)*

This Melchizedek was king of the city of Salem and also a priest of God Most High. When Abraham was returning home after winning a great battle against the kings, Melchizedek met him and blessed him. Then Abraham took a tenth of all he had captured in battle and gave it to Melchizedek. The name Melchizedek means "king of justice", and king of Salem means "king of peace." (Hebrews 7:1-2, NLT; see also Genesis 14:17-24)

Taking a moment to reflect on the training Jesus gave His disciples on finding peace and staying with it. We as Christians can appreciate this guidance too, in our own lives. When sent out among the communities, seventy disciples of Jesus were instructed to first find out if peace was presently dwelling in the homes they visited. If it was there, they had permission granted by Jesus to stay at this particular house. If it were not there, their own peace would return to them. The disciples followed these instructions and the spirit of peace remained with them.

> *"Whatever house you enter, first say, 'Peace be to this house!'*
> *And if a son of peace is there, your peace will rest upon him.*
> *But if not, it will return to you." (Luke 10:5-6, ESV)*

We have the same obligations to follow instructions concerning peace. In order for our own state of tranquility to remain within us, we must not allow the spirit of peace to be stripped away from us. This happens when we are in the midst of forbidden places such as a selfish man's territory, or perhaps an area described in the Bible (Proverbs 33:21-23, NLT) that makes the earth tremble, an odious woman's house. These particular houses can be like hades on earth. If something makes the earth tremble, think of what it can do to us.

The Lord assures us that as the leader and authority in our lives, His presence and guidance are always with us. The more time we spend in prayer and communicating with Christ, the greater our peace will be. Learning from the Word of God gives a greater sense of freedom in times of trouble and danger.

> *"He will cover you with his pinions, and under his wings*
> *you will find refuge; his faithfulness is a shield and buckler.*
> *You will not fear the terror of the night, nor the arrow that*
> *flies by day." (Psalm 91:4-5, ESV)*

UNDERSTANDING THE ROAD

Down the road of traveling grace and mercy is the vicinity of peace. When you make it there, do you know and understand where you are? Are you aware you are in, the midst of God's spirit of peace? Our understanding of this gives us the incentive to obey the rules regarding peace. If we understand where we are, we'll be enthused and much more motivated to accept the information and act accordingly.

The American Christmas classic movie *It's A Wonderful Life* is among the most popular in American cinema because of its numerous television showings. It has become traditional viewing during the Christmas season. The movie is one of the most acclaimed films ever made, praised particularly for its writing. It was nominated for five Academy Awards, including Best Picture. It is recognized as one of the best films ever made.

In the movie, George Bailey is a small-town man whose life looks perfectly bland. He had always dreamed of leaving Bedford Falls, New York to travel to exotic places. Yet, circumstances and his own good heart led him to stay. He sacrificed his education for his brother, kept the family-run savings and loan afloat, and protected the town from the avarice of the greedy banker, Mr. Potter. Fearing that Mr. Potter, the town's richest and meanest man, will have financial control of the town, George agrees to stay and help the people in Bedford Falls.

On Christmas Eve in 1945, George marries his childhood sweetheart, Mary. On this eve, he finds out the bank has called in their business loan. George realizes they have no money, only the honeymoon cash that Mary offers to the customers, which saves the day. George and Mary moved in and made repairs to an old abandoned mansion. This is the same house Mary previously wished for during the night of her graduation dance.

Four children were born, and it felt like it was a wonderful life until the dreadful happened. George's uncle, Harry is to deposit an envelope of $8,000 in the bank, but distracted he accidently puts the money inside Potter's newspaper. Potter does not give the money back and pretends he knows nothing about Harry's loss.

After the loss of the money, George is now on the verge of hysteria over the possibility of bankruptcy and a prison term for embezzlement. He goes home angry and sullen. With his wife preparing for the holiday and the kids enthusiastically enjoying the evening, George disrupts the peace in the house. He is irritated with himself and yelling at everyone including a teacher on the phone he blames for his daughter's flu. He storms out of the house and goes for a drive.

After thinking of his overwhelming problems, he has other plans for this holiday. He is on the verge of suicide and drives to a bridge and gets out of the car. An angel is sent to the earth to keep the despairing

George from killing himself on this crucial night. Just as he is about to jump, a guardian angel named Clarence intercedes by jumping in the water, pretending to drown.

After George saves Clarence, then the angel gives him a glimpse of the future. He shows George what life would have become for the residents of Bedford Falls had he never lived. George prays for forgiveness and his prayers are heard in heaven and peace is restored to him.

Friends and relatives contributed money to make up for the $8,000 loss. George once again had peace in his life. He could continue to help the people of Bedford Falls avoid the stranglehold of Mr. Potter.

This wonderful film reminds us of what's important in this life and why we should keep peace and hope close to us. There is always something good to look forward to even when we are shrouded with that which is fixed against us.

Peace from our Lord Jesus Christ is being ruled in our hearts daily and governed by our Lord and Savior, Jesus Christ. He has the ultimate controlling power over the spirit of peace in our lives. God established the system of peace and how it is to be operated. Christ directs the influence that peace has over situations and conditions. Peace has instructions from God, and these instructions are passed on to you and me by way of operation through the Prince of Peace, Jesus Christ. Peace will always be obedient to God's commands.

> *"Therefore, since we have been made right in God's sight by faith, we have peace with God because of what Jesus Christ our Lord has done for us." (Romans 5:1-2, NLT)*

> *"And let the peace that comes from Christ rule in your hearts. For as members of one body you are called to live in peace. And always be thankful." (Colossians 3:15, NLT)*

THE SPIRIT OF PEACE IS SUBMISSIVE TO GOD

- Peace is obedient to the will of God.
- Peace is not allowed to dwell in, the midst of chaos.
- Peace will be dismissed when chaos shows up.

- Peace will not reside in this same place, house, or life where disorder is welcomed.
- Peace is not permitted to be in the same vicinity or area as evil spirits.
- Peace has no association or contact with any form of evil such as confusion, resentment, anger, envy, hatred, jealousy, gossip, backbiting, lying, maliciousness, or lust.

"Do not bring sorrow to God's Holy Spirit by the way you live. Remember, he has identified you as his own, guaranteeing that you will be saved on the day of redemption. Get rid of bitterness, rage, anger, harsh words, and slander, as well as all types of evil behavior." (Ephesians 4:30-31, NLT)

Our mission in life is to please God and obey His Word. Then we can enjoy benefits of peace in our lives. As we reside with peace, we are able to rest spiritually, mentally, and physically. With peace in the midst, our spirit is free of distress and discomfort. Sorrow and worry are a thing of the past; it is history. The complaining spirit we once had has been buried beneath the sea.

Without being nonchalant, we however, have a chance to be confident and free from the pressure of anything that forces an urgent demand upon us. Let's continue to be free of the forces that cause our spirit to grieve. Let's allow the Lord to keep us safe, comfortable, and content. Let's enjoy the benefits of pursuing peace.

Let us be prayerful and always pay close attention to our surroundings. Be aware of our associations, contacts, and hang out areas. We may have to remove or dismiss ourselves from certain conditions, which affect the presence of peace in our lives. Sometimes, we're the reason peace will leave or won't show up in our lives.

We have an obligation to present our body to God as holy. Our body holds the Spirit of God, and we must present it as a living sacrifice by making sure God and those around us can admire us. Keeping these words in our heart, "Peace will remain with me when I continually present myself worthy to possess the spirit of peace in my life. That is making sure my spoken words, listening ears, and footsteps are all in line with pleasing God."

> *"I appeal to you therefore, brothers, by the mercies of God, to present your bodies as a living sacrifice, holy and acceptable to God, which is your spiritual worship."* (Romans 12:1, ESV)

SUBMISSION REQUIRES PEACE

The spirit of peace is required to be present in order that acts of submission function properly. In order for a person to be in full submission to their overseer, there must be peace in the midst. Peace is required to be present for the good of the arrangement. During tumultuous and rocky times in our life, God will fight our battles when we remain at rest.

The psalmist stresses in the Bible the importance of having a close relationship with God, through Jesus Christ: *"When the righteous cry for help, the Lord hears and delivers them out of all their trouble"* (Psalm 34:17, EVS).

Having peace in, the midst of our lives means we're crucifying the flesh of immoral desires. This may not be an easy task for some, but it can be done. Help from our Lord, Jesus Christ assists us in being supportive to the authority given to the spirit of peace, to then control our lives. When peace is in the midst, this prevents us from provoking one another and stirring up resentment. Being submissive to the Word of God is the only way society can live in harmony among one another. May we continue on in the spirit of peace.

"Peace does not mean an absence of conflict; differences will always be there. Peace means solving these differences through peaceful means; through dialogue, education, knowledge; and through humane ways." (Dalai Lama XIV)

> In the book of Galatians, Paul writes, *"They that are Christ's have crucified the flesh with the affections and lusts. If we live by the Spirit, let us also keep in step with the Spirit. Let us not become conceited, provoking one another, envying one another"* (Galatians 5:25, ESV).

CHAPTER 7

THE FIRST WOMAN

"But the Lord is faithful, and he will strengthen you and protect you from the evil one." (2 Thessalonians 3:3, NIV)

Women today, like the first woman of the Bible, Eve, have specific orders from God concerning submission. These orders are a bit more complex than those orders of the men. The order pertaining to women concerning submission is different in that women have an additional overseer—this extra coverage being her husband or spiritual leader.

Unlike men, women are protected against the liabilities of certain risks. Those liabilities are the unfavorable confrontations of the enemy. For instance, we can compare this additional coverage women have to children that are under their parents' control until they reach a certain age. A slight difference of course, the women remain in this position for their own spiritual protection.

In reading Genesis, we can see this order became effective in the Garden of Eden during Adam and Eve's time. The mind is a battleground and Satan, is always ready to go against the knowledge of God. Females are commanded by God to be in submission to their husband's authority. This authority is a shield for women to use against ungodly thoughts, which leads to wicked behavior and in the end, spiritual death.

The first woman, Eve, was a well-known female figure of the Bible and came under strict and specific obligations to submit to her husband because of a weakness. That weakness was the serpent easily influenced her. Eve was the first human to be attacked by the enemy and certainly not the last. Through her weakness, she was totally deceived by the devil. This enemy of God (Satan) persuaded her to go against a spiritual order of obedience God had previously set before Adam and Eve. This interchange of thoughts was a battleground of the minds between Eve and the Serpent. Was she prepared for this spiritual war? Apparently not. She allowed the enemy of God to control her mind, therefore controlling her actions.

The order of obedience given directly by God was that she and Adam were not to eat from this particular tree. It was originally designed as a priestly role for Adam to protect the sanctuary of the Garden of Eden. God's design was also to teach Adam and Even between right and wrong. God expected the two of them to keep His commandments and care for His creation.

> *"The Lord God warned him (Adam), 'You may freely eat the fruit of every tree in the garden – except the tree of the knowledge of good and evil. If you eat its fruit, you are sure to die.'" (Genesis 2:16, NLT)*

See also Genesis 3, where the serpent (devil) entices Eve by lying to her. Satan lied to her saying she will not die if she ate from the Tree of Knowledge. She allowed the devil to alter her thoughts about God. This weakness of Eve began through her ears and they became soft. She heard words from the serpent that were different from the words God had given. Unknown to her as lies, Eve perceived the words of the serpent to be worth listening.

In reading Genesis, we become aware of Adam's role in this extremely severe test. Let's keep our focus on Eve. Because of her curiosity, the devil was able to convince Eve that this beautiful tree would give her the same knowledge God has. She gave attention to the serpent and acted on this lie. Eve willingly disobeyed God and went along with the serpent's plan. She took of the fruit from the tree ate it and gave some to her husband Adam and he ate it, too. The eyes of Adam and Eve were opened knowing good and evil.

> *"And Adam was not deceived, but the woman being deceived was in the transgression." (1 Timothy 2:14, KJV)*

"I am afraid that as the serpent deceived Eve by his cunning, your thoughts will be led astray from a sincere and pure devotion to Christ." (2 Corinthians 11:3, ESV)

"The serpent is later referred in the Bible as Satan. And he seized the dragon, that ancient serpent, who is the devil and Satan." (Revelation 20:2a, ESV)

Taking a closer look at her situation, it appears at this point Eve is out of control. She was not capable of thinking clearly about the consequences. Why? Because she was out of the boundary of God's will. While out there, she's in Satan's territory. At this point, he had control of her mind and he can probably get her to do almost anything. He manipulated her into thinking the fruit is a gift. She anxiously satisfies her fleshly craving by eating from the forbidden tree.

After being caught in her wrongdoing, Eve was not willing to admit she was wrong. She immediately placed the blame of her disobedience on the serpent. She was reprimanded by God and punished for her decision to disobey His order. Although Eve suffered from a form of weakness, she was still held accountable for her actions. Eve's husband, Adam, and the serpent were also punished for their roles as well. (See Genesis 3:17-19.)

The Apostle Paul explains the man Adam was not the one deceived, but the woman Eve in her transgression. Adam chose to sin against God. In Eve's transgression, she was in a state beyond God's boundaries. Her disrespect for God's commands was at a point where she violated the will of God, got Adam to do the same. The position of Eve's thoughts about God made it easy for the serpent to deceive her, and that he did.

Being curious by nature, Eve's emotions were easily stimulated. She was excessively eager to know if God was lying to them about death. Eve's sense of judgment was way off balance because she was out in Satan's territory. Her ability to make a wise decision was diminished. Could this human weakness be a psychological defect as well as a spiritual defect? Unfortunately, I'm not a doctor and can't answer this question. As my doctor often tells me, "That's a $64,000 question."

EVE'S REPERCUSSIONS

Eve's judgment from God was one that every woman after her would experience. Even in God's judgment in this matter, we can see His mercy as he blesses her with children. *"Behold children are a heritage from the Lord, the fruit of the womb a reward" (Psalm 127:3, ESV).* Before she was blessed, Eve's suffered the repercussions of her disobedience.

- The words God said to Eve (Genesis 3:16 (NIV):

"I will make your pains in childbearing very severe;"

There will be a great increase in her expressions of grief during pregnancy.

"With painful labor, you will give birth to children."

In this sorrow that Eve experiences, she will express great distress during her labor of bring forth children to the world. She will suffer a large amount of pain and emotional distress and she will express this pain.

- *"Your desire will be for your husband, and he will rule over you."*

Eve's desire would be directed toward her husband, and he will be the focus of her interest and attention. Her requests and all of her needs are aimed toward her husband. He rules over her in that he will have spiritual authority over her. He will have a powerful influence in the decisions of her everyday life. God has moved her to this position of submission.

EVE HAS A MANAGER

A Gallup survey examining over 27 million employees found that female managers are more engaged than their male counterparts. During this study, they found that the females occupied more effort than the males as employees and female bosses were more involved with their employees. These numbers aren't brilliant, but a distinction is there with the highest pledge of numbers from female employees.

The report also says women's higher engagement level likely resulted in more engaged and higher-performing teams. Despite women's outstanding contributions, they oftentimes feel overlooked when it comes to pay and equality in the workforce. As they work alongside men, they feel some bosses do not recognize them nor are they compensated as well as their male colleagues.

The Bible speaks of several women who played major roles in the ministry of Jesus. It was a female who first saw Jesus after his resurrection. He first appeared to Mary Magdalene and by nature, she clung to Him. He then instructed her to go and tell His disciples that He is ascending to His Father. Jesus used a woman to initiate the good news of His resurrection. An old saying: "If you want something told, tell a woman." Mary did just as she was instructed. Jesus' resurrection is proof of who He claims to be: The Son of God. (See this account in John 20:11-18.)

Mary Magdalene was the first to be commissioned by Jesus. He commissioned her to go and share what she had just witnessed. Jesus has risen from the grave and He is alive. Jesus showed He trusted Mary and He showed that women are an important part of mankind. He showed He did not limit women to silence or hold them in the background unseen and unheard. The same holds true for women today.

The world holds some of the most successful entrepreneurs of our generation. They are just as trustworthy as Mary Magdalene. Many have been given authority for a certain function. Many of these women are talked about often. If there's one person whose name is the subject of household dinner, it's one of these powerful entrepreneurs. They have been trusted to many tasks. These women have aligned their personality with their determination. As powerful as these women are, even some of them need an overseer, someone to look after their spiritual character.

A woman's occupation and profession can sometimes be controlled by her decision to maintain her career. Those not under the authority of a leader is trying to control their own interest. They have adopted a masculine trait in order to get the job done. I'm not saying a masculine trait is not a part of submission, because men are masculine. Yet, for a woman with masculine traits, it means she's trying to handle things on her own and not allowing God's way to rule her life.

When it comes to her spiritually, Eve was given a manager. Why? Because God saw fit that she, based on her conversion with the enemy, needed an overseer. God decided to use Adam as the overseer and he would direct his wife's spiritual character. Not only was she the first human to be attacked by Satan, she was also the first human to be placed under spiritual protection. Eve proved to God that she does not have the ability to handle her own spirituality and protection. As a result of her behavior, God placed her in a submissive position under her husband, Adam. This move was for her sake. With the exception of unlimited power, Adam had the position of overseer to take charge of her affairs. God chose him to act as her manager.

Adam must submit entirely to God's will and walk confidently in His Word. Eve's spiritual life was dependent upon him. He would direct the everyday affairs of himself and his wife, especially her contact with the serpent. He would maintain control of his wife's interest and curiosity using the skills provided by God. We can be sure that if God placed Adam in this position, he equipped him with the necessary skills to handle certain issues pertaining to his wife and her performances. Adam had power by God to protect Eve as she worked on being a godly woman.

There were issues involving Eve's curiosity, which moved God to place her in a position of submission under her husband. Curiosity is when a person has a desire and interest in knowing about something. I think that interest can sometimes be easily excited to a point of eagerness. I also think any interest aroused to a degree higher than that considered normal is like an out-of-control craving.

For instance, a diabetic has cravings for sugar and a child craves to play outside. Eve did not have the ability to restrain herself. Her fleshly desires had escalated far above her reach to restrain herself. She craved to know if God was lying to them about death and this certain tree.

> *"Walk by the Spirit, and you will not gratify the desires of the flesh. For the desires of the flesh are against the Spirit,*

and the desires of the Spirit are against the flesh, for these are opposed to each other, to keep you from doing the things you want to do." (Galatians 5:16-17, ESV)

Like Eve, all women have a natural tendency in wanting to know things, including the things that are of no concern to them. For some, this curiosity can cause them to be entangled into situations and circumstances beyond their control. For this reason, a manager may be a necessity. This heightened sense of curiosity is a shortcoming for women and must be worked on daily.

The same thing that happened to the first woman, Eve, in the Garden of Eden, is still happening today to females across the globe. It's happening on a moment-to-moment basis every day. Oppositions to God's Word present themselves as truths and there is a constant struggle to remain within the boundary of God's will. A spiritual manager is then needed. For those without a direct manager or husband, a willing heart to be obedient to the will of God is essential.

"Do you not know that your body is a temple of the Holy Spirit within you, whom you have from God? You are not your own, for you were bought with a price. So, glorify God in your body." (1 Corinthians 6:19-20, ESV)

Paul's advice to those who are single: *"I say to those who aren't married and to widows – it is better to stay unmarried, just as I am. But if they can't control themselves, they should go ahead and marry. It's better to marry than to burn with lust." (1 Corinthians 7:8, NLT)*

Whether married or single, women should always be attentive to the original signs and symbols of this weakness mentioned earlier:

- The interest of a woman is awakened through the auditory.
- Emotions then stir to an arousal state.
- These feelings can sometimes be soothing and comforting.
- The feelings can also be irritating and uncomfortable.

- Uncomfortable emotions can stimulate her to action.
- The actions taken during the latter arousal state can sometimes result in behavior that is sporadic and unattractive.
- The consequences are usually a dangerous out-of-control situation, which the woman can't get herself out of.

The end result, when problems arise, such as those posed by Eve, the best interest of the woman lies under the direct leadership and authority of her husband or other spiritual leaders. If she is unmarried or unaware of the enemy's signs, she must seek the Lord's guidance every day, in everything and everyway. Implying here she must live through God's Word, praying without ceasing, and surrounding herself with godly leaders and other Christian women. Because deception is the primary means of leading many to rebel against God's order.

> "Guard me, O Lord, from the hands of the wicked; preserve me from violent men, who have planned to trip up my feet ... I say to the Lord, You are my God; give ear to the voice of my pleas for mercy, O Lord!" (Psalm 139:4-6, ESV)

God saw fit that for the sake of the woman, she is safer with this extra covering He offers (the husband and other spiritual leaders being that coverage). She is safe from different sources that strongly provokes her curiosity and excites her to a higher degree causing her emotions to become out of control. This order is set in order that the behaviors of the woman may remain within the boundaries of God's will.

Can the woman still make decisions concerning her family? Absolutely. Can she still manage the household finances? Yes, indeed she can. Does she have a say-so in personal issues? Yes. Can she ask questions and give her husband advice? Yes. All of this is done as she humbly submits to the leadership of her husband the same way she submits to the Lord.

Not with a domineering attitude of course, the husband and other spiritual leaders will manage her way of thinking. This coverage is a blessing for the woman. She can achieve this blessing by having consideration and understanding that this way is proper for her own spiritual wellbeing. Her husband and spiritual managers work closely with her on a daily basis for the sake of her soul.

While married, the wife submitting to her husband means she is confident that her husband will please God before any attempts to satisfy her emotions. She remains relaxed and comfortable in the confidence she has in God. Whether she is married or single, her God-given duty is to accept her husband and/or spiritual leaders and submit to them as she submits to the Lord. She can rejoice because she has a greater chance at spiritual success.

In some religious cultures around the world, women are not allowed to use verbal expressions while in presence of men in public. Jesus, on the other hand, lifted up women to be respectfully equal. His interactions with women are important to the debate about Christianity and women. In many stories surrounding Jesus, women are well known and noticeable.

Jesus was born of a woman and throughout His ministry He showed consideration for women. Women became His disciples and they were undoubtedly protected while under His leadership. Right before Jesus died, he beseeched John to take care of His mother, which meant John would become her spiritual leader. Jesus knew the dangers she would face after He was gone. He made sure she was covered before went on to his father's mansion *(See this account in John 19:25-27).*

> *"Wives, submit to your own husbands, as to the Lord."*
> *(Ephesians 5:22, ESV)*

CHAPTER 8

TARGET OF SATAN

"But the Lord is faithful, and he will strengthen you and protect you from the evil one." (2 Thessalonians 3:3, NIV)

The spiritual and physical lives of all of us, men and women alike, are protected and saved when following God's order. His order serves as a life preserver, especially for those whom Satan has chosen as a target. There are some prone to fall prey to the deception and lies of this evil one. Why? Because there is a natural inclination to flow along with things, not knowing whether such things are perfect or flawless. A vast majority becomes an easy target for Satan to mislead because true deception is not always easy to discern.

This imperfection is what Satan uses when he targets people for an attack. With Christ Jesus being a perfect individual, He was even tempted by this evil spirit, Satan. The enemy's attempt was to draw Jesus away from His path of perfect obedience to God's will. Since all believers are tempted in a similar way, society can learn a lot from the temptations of Christ. We can learn how to stand firm on God's Word in the face of the enemy.

"Then Jesus was led up by the Spirit into the wilderness to be tempted by the devil. And after fasting forty days and forty nights, he was hungry. And the tempter came and said to him, *"If you are the Son of God, command these stones to become loaves of bread."* But he (Jesus) answered, *"It is by every word that comes from the mouth of God.""* (Matthew 4:1-4, ESV)

After fasting for forty days and forty nights, Jesus was hungry. Satan then tried to take advantage Him while He was physically weak from hunger. Jesus used the Word of God as a weapon against this temptation. He defeated Satan by the power invested to Him by God. Jesus stood up to Satan and was not about to let the enemy change the course of God's survival plan for humanity. This plan was set to introduce and present God's kingdom to the world, destroy the works of Satan, and free us from the control of the evil one.

"*"Get out of here, Satan," Jesus told him. 'For the Scriptures say, You must worship the Lord your God and serve only him.'"* (Matthew 4:10, NLT)

There was a period in my life where I was a direct target of Satan. Like Eve, he put things into my mind about God and myself that were simply untrue. This enemy of God tried to manipulate and control my mind to a point of no return. On one day, I'll never forget, Lord showed me I was in a large dark and crowded pit; I was screaming and crying, reaching for my mother's hand, so she can pull me out, but she couldn't get to me.

It would have been an awesome thing to be as strong as Jesus, but I wasn't. I became suicidal; even with my mother praying, the question whether God sincerely loved me remained. My thoughts were, if God was there, He didn't like what I had become; an object being bombarded by the enemy. I no longer had interest to continue, on earth and wanted to die. The pain associated with the thoughts was more than I could handle.

Although depression was present, there were other contributing factors to why I thought of taking my own life. A victim of sexual abuse as a teenager at the hands of a doctor heightened the process. I was fourteen-years-old, my parents had taken me for a first-time gynecology appointment. My father was in the waiting room and mother was sitting in the doctor's office awaiting results of the exam. After the ordeal, I was immediately overwhelmed with feelings of despair and sadness.

It was difficult to seek help because I felt there was no one I could trust with the torment I had just experienced. Certainly, couldn't tell Dad what had just happened because he would most definitely end up in jail. My thoughts were, "What would happen to mom and her baby boomers?" It was 1975 and most of mom's children were still much dependent upon her and dad. As the years went by, the Lord still blessed me along the way. Still, there was this struggle going on between the love in my heart for God and the control Satan wanted of my mind. My love for God was being smothered by an overwhelming sensation to end it all.

Raising four children alone as a divorced mom required great labor. Having to shift back and forth from being mother to father bewildered not only the kids, but me too. There were overwhelming feelings of hopelessness and at times I felt inadequate as a parent.

Besides the overpowering stages that happened in my life, I began to dangerously date men who were obviously not a harmony for me, nor good for my descendants who depended upon me. Here, living this life style I felt this one reason God was not pleased with me. I knew deep down inside this probably wasn't a good route to take, but I just couldn't see the light at the end of the tunnel.

> *"For among them are those who creep into households and capture weak women, burdened with sins and led astray by various passions, always learning and never able to arrive at a knowledge of the truth." (2 Timothy 3:6-7, ESV)*

After the sexual and physical abuse, submitting to someone in authority was an issue for me because, I trusted no one. Those with a license and ones delegated with authorization to act in power were the ones in whom I had no confidence. The fear of having someone in control of me or my body was overwhelming. I was afraid of possibly being abused again. This was one of my shortcomings I dealt with, and this one lasted over thirty years.

Back then, this is the way I perceived things: if you can't trust those who are supposed to facilitate your progress in life, who can you trust? I wasn't about to submit to a leader other than me, myself, and I. Not knowing this was a disservice to my spiritual life, I refused to be under the controlling authority of anyone, including another husband. So, I chose to remain single for the next thirty years. I felt there was not one soul on earth I could trust with my life, especially men.

Even though my trust in God was diminished due to negative circumstances, God still blessed me along the way. He found ways to keep that fire, my parents lit, burning inside of me. I found out years later that His love for me never changed. The Lord was still showing me signs of His loyalty and affection. At the same time, the enemy's influence was still clouding the direction of my freedom. Free to love God without any doubt, free to be living a life that God approved of. Having an IQ of 147 was not enough to stabilize and sustain my life. It was not enough for me to free myself from the enemy of God obliging me with all sorts of accusations against God.

Satan had a field day with my afflictions and mental sufferings. His cunning ways were to change my perception of God. He wanted my soul and he would not give up. He tried and tried again to convince me that my life was not worth living and the only way out was death.

For years, I kept this torment of Satan and the sexual abuse to myself. No one knew of the pain I experienced. Part of the pain was the memory of what happened in that doctor's office years ago. It was, however, still etched in my mind. I was uncomfortable with life so, I moved around a lot. Back and forth, from state to state with my kids in tow. Didn't realize it at the time how important stability was for my children. Didn't realize the impact that changing our locations so often would have on them.

When I was about thirty-five-years-old, gathered my two youngest children and moved hundreds of miles up north to Minneapolis, Minnesota. I tried to get away from all the noise in my head. We moved in with my sister and her kids temporarily until I could find job and housing for us. Within about three weeks of being here, things weren't working out at my sister's house and she told me we had to leave. Without going into details of my sister's lifestyle, I'll just say, I, along with my daughters, immediately became homeless in this new and strange city.

It was the middle of winter and snowing; there was two feet of snow on the ground and the temperature was below zero. With the wind chill, that made the temperature even lower. It was getting dark and the streetlights had just come on. The only thing moving around outside in this frozen city was the wind. There was nowhere for us to go. The homeless shelter was our only option. A blizzard was in the forecast and it predicted twelve inches of snow would fall within the next twenty-four hours. The wintry weather was upon us.

We packed up the little belongings we had and left my sister's house. As we walked to the car, we could see our breath crystalize before our eyes. We drove to the only refuge that would protect us from frostbite, the women's shelter located on the other side of the Mississippi River in St. Paul. While driving on Freeway 94, the car was quiet, and for me, homelessness had started to settle in.

Upon our arrival at the shelter, they gave us blankets and a warm room to stay. It was temporary housing until we located permanent residency. We took our luggage upstairs and sat quietly in the room. The girls probably wondered what was going on. I explained this was just temporary until we found a place to stay.

I felt the need to do some thinking, but the freezing cold overcame my desire to go for a walk. So, I stood in front of the mirror and it showed that I had hit rock bottom. One of the many sleepless nights at the shelter, I awoke and starred out the window of the shelter. It was obvious that the whole city was shut down. I wondered to myself, *"how on earth did I end up here?"*

GOD WILL NEVER FORSAKE US

"Never will I leave you; never will I forsake you." (Hebrews 13:5b, NIV)

The next morning, a paper flyer on the wall of the shelter caught my eye. Counseling services were being offered in St. Paul, not far from the shelter. I signed up and immediately began counseling sessions. Tons of paperwork had to be filled out and several tests done, including an IQ test. The psychologist and psychiatrist assigned to me were nice and easy to talk to. The never-ending patience of the psychologist is what won me over to remain at the clinic.

The Lord began to work through this counselor and she began to work on me. She encouraged me, as painful as it was, to lay my entire life out on the table. The good, the bad, and the ugly. With the tears rolling down my face, it was as if the pain had started yesterday. The shame of it all was now out in the open. I was thirty-five years old and had never seen a professional of this sort. The first session started twenty years after the turmoil had begun in my life. Even then, I knew Mom still prayed.

The Lord sometimes allows us to be brought to the end of our strength so that we may utter a call to Him for relief. Will I continue in my sufferings because I'm this independent woman handling things my way? Or, will I trust in Jesus and depend on Him to order my footsteps and control my life?

> Jesus said, *"The thief's purpose is to steal and kill and destroy. My purpose is to give them a rich and satisfying life"* (John 10:10, NLT).

> *"After you have suffered a little while, the God of all grace, who has called you to his eternal glory in Christ, will himself restore, confirm, strengthen, and establish you. To Him be the dominion forever and ever. Amen."* (1 Peter 5:10-11, ESV)

This conflict with Satan had been going on for years. There was no way I could continue to fight in this battlefield alone. I desperately needed the Lord. My daughters and I eventually moved back to Louisiana. It would take another eight years after the counseling sessions in St. Paul before I saw the light.

Moving forward. One day in 2004, I went to my mother's house and sought her help on how to get my life back on track. As always, she kept the conversation strictly on God and His love for me. She helped me to come, to a realization that I needed supernatural help from the Lord. Mom told me, "Turn it loose and give it God because this is the only way you're going to get some ease."

The consequences of my own violation of God's Word had formed my life to one that was indescribable. The agony of it all was horrific.

A few days after the talk with Mom, it was a quiet afternoon and I was home alone. Reflecting on the words of my mother, I took heed to her advice. Picked up my Bible and began reading God's Word. With the Bible in my hands, I got down on my knees, poured out my heart to God. I literally cried out to God saying, "Lord, I can't continue on like this, I desperately need your help. I don't want to live another day like this; either you help me now or please let me come home. Help me! Please, Lord! Help me!"

The Lord heard my cry; He immediately reached out and touched my soul. A sense of calmness came over me because I heard a voice I could trust. A voice which I hadn't heard in a long time. The Lord said to me, "You can relax, I am with you. I will never leave you." I instantly knew He set me free of Satan's control.

On this day, the Lord blessed me, gave me a new heart, and a meaningful life through a personal relationship with Him. He lifted me from that dark pit, took over my thoughts, and restored my mind. I was overwhelmed with joy and appreciation of His love.

I was amused by His love and compassion. I became interested and anxious in non-other than the things of God's kingdom. Made a promise to follow Jesus in everything. Up to that point, I didn't have a church home, but spent every day in God's Word, vigorously studying and praying throughout the day. I gave my mother of course the good news of my renewed relationship with Christ. With a smile on her face and her palms raised in praise to God, she said, "Hallelujah, thank you Jesus!" She knew the Lord had answered her prayers.

Sometime around 2006, the Lord began to direct my attention to connect with a certain church, a large congregation, this was out of my comfort zone. I wasn't used to such large crowds of people. Another two years would pass before I was obedient to Him. Only after the Lord gave me a lecture in my kitchen one afternoon. I obeyed. That following Sunday, my daughter and I got dressed and went to First Baptist Church of West Monroe, Louisiana. A short time later we joined church, and both were baptized. This time I had a clear understanding of my public declaration of being an obedient follower of Jesus Christ.

Today, my interests and desires have not wavered, they remain with Christ. I tend to be interested only in conversations about God, Jesus Christ, and the Holy Spirit. Social conversations going on daily are of no interest to me. The books I read are all related to spiritual things. This became a preference the day the Lord saved my life and renewed my mind.

It is so awesome and inspiring to be in the presence of God's Holy Spirit. Sometimes, I can feel when the power of God is upon me; there's a clinging sensation in the top of my head and it captures my undivided attention. I believe this is a reminder from the Lord that the Holy Spirit is alive and with me always. The sensation is like a sprouting water fountain that had been turned on. As the Holy Spirit flourishes, I savor the moment, close my eyes, listen, and with my palms raised, give God the praise. "Hallelujah, thank you Jesus!"

In His infinite wisdom, God will always choose a way for us to obtain salvation through Jesus Christ. About a year after I dedicated my life to the Lord, He spoke to me and said, "Hold out your hands."

I did as he asked and said, "Yes, Lord I'm here."

He then said, "I will bless the hands that take these hands." The tears began to flow because I knew His prophecy would someday come true.

> "Then they cried to the Lord in their trouble, and he delivered them from their distress. He made the storm be still, and the waves of the sea were hushed. Then they were glad that the waters were quiet, and he brought them to their desired haven." (Psalm 107:28-30, ESV)

In March 2010, I had an opportunity, along with nine other Christian women, to visit the country of Israel. This trip left a lasting impression upon me. Walking some of the same routes Jesus took while on Earth was an overpowering amusement.

It gives you a glimpse of life as it happened in the New Testament of the Bible. Places like Jerusalem, Bethlehem, Nazareth, The Western

Wall, Sea of Galilee, and the Dead Sea are all part of this fascinating country.

While in Israel, a few of the women on this tour including myself were baptized in the Jordan River. This is the same river where John the Baptist had baptized Jesus some two thousand years ago. The same river where God immediately spoke from Heaven after Jesus was baptized and said, *"This is my beloved Son, with whom I am well pleased"* (*Matthew 3:16-17, ESV*). The country of Israel has an area roughly located between the Jordan River and the Mediterranean Sea known as The Holy Land. It is said to be the most sacred place on earth and when you go there, you'll understand why. It is Holy ground.

Another blessing I am pleased to announce is when the Lord again bestowed favor upon me on August 10, 2013. Thirty years after my divorce and living a single life, God provided a loving husband whom I honor and submit to in the Lord. Brian is a kind and wonderful man; he prays with me, for our family, and for others on, a daily basis. He is constantly being fed with the reading of God's Word. Brian is truly a gift from God. Absolutely indeed, he helps to manage my way of thinking. We are both blessed beyond measure to have each other.

Brian picked me up from work and we went to lunch at Fuddruckers World's Greatest Hamburgers. Little did I know, he had an engagement ring in his pocket. He got down on one knee where we sat, in front of a large lunch crowd, and proposed to me. At that moment, I knew God had fulfilled His promise. After thirty years of singleness I said "Yes". An elderly gentleman sitting alone and nearby, he smiled and gave me a thumb's up. When I go back to the office with my left hand raised and palm facing me, my coworkers were surprised. My boss said, "I thought you were going to the bank." I said with a big smile, "I did go, right before lunch." Six months later Brian and I said our vows.

As we stood before the altar to be married, surrounded by our children and grandkids, you could feel the presence of the Holy Spirit. Right before the ceremony started, Brian looked into my eyes and took hold of my hands. He held them during the entire ceremony. I couldn't hold back the tears because I remembered the Lord's promise to me some nine years earlier. When the Lord speaks of His promises, He will always come through for us. This current year is 2017 and I'm looking forward to visiting Israel again in November. This time, hand-in-hand with my husband Brian.

> *"Praise the Lord! Oh, give thanks to the Lord, for he is good,*
> *for his steadfast love endures forever." (Psalm 106:1, ESV)*

Today, by the grace of God I am a living testimony that God is real, and He loves us unconditionally. I am no longer ashamed of my testimony because God has removed the shame. He receives all the glory for my travels. As my entire attention is devoted to serving the Lord, I search for the highest purpose for which God created me. The waters of my mind are quiet, and the waves of the sea are hushed. I am free and grateful to the Lord because He is in control of my entire being.

The Lord is forever changing lives. With sovereignty, He rules over all He has created. His wisdom transcends above the knowledge of angels and humans. He reveals Himself to all those who long to see Him. Every promise that God has made to man will come to pass because He honors His every word.

When observing my surroundings, I am always reminded of God's power and what He has done in my life. The misfortune that had been invoked upon me by Satan was reversed by the wonder working powers of God. Satan could not dismantle my foundation, the foundation built by my parents, decades ago. God's blessings and grace are forever with me. In turn, I trust in His ability to control my life and turn any difficult situation around. I truly thank Him for His steadfast love.

No matter who we are, whether an influential genius or a dull-witted person, we will never be independent of God's presence and impression in our lives. We may try, but at the end of the day, we will somehow realize we do indeed need God in our life. Old or young, rich or poor, we will always and forever require close association with Him.

> *"I love you, Lord, my strength.*
> *The Lord is my rock, my fortress and my deliverer;*
> *My God is my rock, in whom I take refuge,*
> *My shield and the horn of my salvation, my stronghold.*
> *I called to the Lord who is worthy of praise.,*

And I have been saved from my enemies.
The cords of death entangled me;
The torrents of destruction overwhelmed me.
The cords of the grave coiled around me;
The snares of death confronted me.
In my distress, I called to the Lord;
I cried to my God for help.
From his temple, he heard my voice;
My cry came before him, into his ears."
(Psalm 18:1-6, NIV)

—— C H A P T E R 9 ——

COPING WITH ADVERSITY

"When Jesus spoke again to the people, he said, 'I am the light of the world. Whoever follows me will never walk in darkness, but will have the light of life.'" (John 8:12, NIV)

According to the United States Food and Drug Administration, there are about 43,000 suicides in America each year. The regulatory and guidance information on Suicidal Ideation and Behavior stated an estimated 8.3 million adults reported having suicidal thoughts. Experts believe there may be a genetic factor associated with a higher risk of suicide. Individuals with suicidal thoughts, or those who have taken their own lives tend to have a family history of suicide or suicidal thoughts.

The most common situations of life events that might cause suicidal thoughts are grief, sexual abuse, financial problems, rejection, and relationship problems. It can happen to anyone at any given time. Some of the most influential people are suicidal or have taken their own lives. Many people have suicidal thoughts and they have never told a soul about their intentions and/or actions. If you are one of those people, hang in there and say these words:

1. No matter how bad things may seem, I will never lose hope.
2. I may not be there yet, but I'm closer than I was yesterday.
3. Someday, everything will make perfect sense.
4. So, for now I will laugh at confusion and smile through the tears.
5. I will always stay strong.

We can be thankful there are a number of treatment options available for those in need of help. There are many centers in the United States where one can receive aid in the fight against suicidal ideation and suicide. Although centers can help, they are not the ultimate cure for the displaced soul collapsing in despair.

Adversity comes in many forms of grievous afflictions. I think these afflictions can inhibit our progress of submitting totally to God and depending upon Him in everything. These afflictions are what Satan uses when he attacks, a believer. When we go through pain, grief, distress, and misery, we are at our weakest. This is like an open door for the enemy to attack.

There are unfavorable misfortunes that seem to follow some people throughout life. In my case, as some others, there was a dire need to have an intervention of the Holy Spirit in order to be freed of Satan's plan of destruction. The enemy targeting me would not have ended unless the Lord stepped in to intervene. A loving relationship with the Lord is the only thing that saved my physical and spiritual life.

> "What is impossible with people is possible with God." (Luke 18:27, NLT)

As I walk closer and closer with the Lord, I can see from experience when the enemy is overtaking a person. The Lord has allowed me to see things I've never seen before. Effective prayers for that person are on my heart as the Lord begins to speak to me about this battleground for prayer. I listen intently and realize the Lord is speaking to me in an expressive way. At that moment, He is requesting I step up without a lapse in time, as a warrior, and pray on behalf of this person.

It's a sad thing to see this happen to anyone, especially those closest to you. At that moment, there is nothing earthly you can do except pray for this person. In honoring the Lord's work, I immediately pray and sometimes ask for an intervention from the Holy Spirit to redeem them back to normal conditions. I thank Christ Jesus our Lord who has given me encouragement along with strength to do His will. It's an honor and enjoyable experience.

At this present day and time, we must all realize that, like Jesus and Eve, we too can still be tempted by Satan. Accepting our own imperfection will allow us room to accept the will of God and help us remember our spiritual guide, Jesus Christ, is always there. The conclusion is we must remain under the controlling power of our Lord for the sake of our spiritual success.

Let's not forget there's a spiritual warfare going on and as followers of Jesus Christ, let's always be prayerful as we help those in need. Take refuge in the Lord and look to Him for guidance. Pray constantly for God's help in recognizing the attempts of Satan in order to avoid his deceptions. God promises to come near to all who pursue His guidance. This safety and protection will save the lives of many.

> *"When you go through rivers of difficulty, you will not drown. When you walk through the fire of oppression, you will not be burned up; the flames will not consume you. For I am the Lord, your God, the Holy One of Israel, your Savior." (Isaiah 43:2-3a, NLT)*

SAFE FROM THE BOUNDARY LINE

Men are not excluded from submission. They have the same obligation to submit to every Word of God. At this moment, let's take an additional glance at the temptations of women. Keep in mind the boundary we discussed earlier. I particularly stress the importance of tracking, through God's Word, the ramifications of being lured into Satan's territory. Knowing the strategies of the enemy will give you an upper hand at preventing an attack. Pray and ask the Lord for wisdom and understanding on this subject. Search the Scriptures and allow the Holy Spirit to guide you through the process of discovering truths.

We've seen over the years that women are strong in many ways and capable of handling difficult dilemmas. Although, several women have proven to be exceptionally powerful and courageous, some are not conscious of the fact they are inclined to be a direct target of Satan's attacks. The devil's attempt is to get as many people as he can to cross the boundary line set by God. On the contrary, there is spiritual guidance available in many sources. Like Jesus, speaking the Word of God over every situation is an effective weapon.

> "Husbands, live with your wives in an understanding way, showing honor to the woman as the weaker vessel, since they are heirs with you of the grace of life, so that your prayers may not be hindered." (1 Peter 3:7, ESV)

We must admit, as the first woman Eve, women are the weaker vessel and naturally vulnerable to the dangers of this world. In the Bible, the Apostle Peter elaborates on this subject as he speaks to the husbands. The enemy takes a wide stance with his target in sight aiming at any weak vessel in sight, oftentimes hitting the target head on.

If the woman is married, the husband, having Christ-like love for his wife, sends a message to the enemy this woman is off limits. The enemy then realizes he must go through the man to get to her. Satan's unlikely target vanishes before his sight. The husband does this by remaining close to the Lord as he covers his wife spiritually.

If a woman is not married, she must personally follow the specific guidelines in the Bible of a godly woman for her safety. At the same time, if she is unable to control issues pertaining to her nature she must pray and ask God for a spiritual leader, someone who will give her spiritual counsel and guidance when needed. She too can have the spiritual guidance and protection as if she was married, only if she follows the guiding principles of acquiring certain qualities.

In addition, help is available from the spiritual leaders and other Christians with spiritual gifts from the Lord. These gifts are available to assist in many different situations. The spiritual help is just as effective as if she were married. Some leaders have distinctive gifts provided to them by the Holy Spirit. They have the same authority and ability to steer her on the path that God has designed for her life. Depending on the severity of issues involved, some contacts need two or more guiding leaders.

The ways in which a woman reveals her nature in connection with the will of God are set within certain guidelines. A woman's highest position, privilege, and true feminine dignity are as godly women. This position may be a leader in the women's ministry or as wife directly under her husband's leadership. Accepting the spiritual roles assigned to us by our Creator, women will experience no greater joy and contentment. This, in turn, brings honor and glory to our Lord, Jesus Christ.

"Houses and wealth are inherited from fathers, but a prudent wife is from the Lord." (Proverbs 19:14, ESV)

"An excellent wife is the crown of her husband but she who brings shame is like rottenness in his bones." (Proverbs 12:4, ESV)

The Apostle Paul mentions during a woman's childbearing years, she is saved from touching the boundary line. The attacks of Satan are minimized. During pregnancy and rearing of children, women are safe from the cunnings Satan uses to excite her. With her husband as her overseer, her mind and heart are occupied. She is filled with love and her attention is toward her husband and children. What happens if she has no children or they have all left the nest? She must accept, and endure without opposition, the same qualities of a godly woman.

The childbearing years are at the beginning of the training program and good for practice. During these years, most of the time a woman's interest and the focus of her heart and mind are on her husband and children, not likely to be out in Satan's territory where he can influence. Her desires remain in a safe zone; this is where she should be, twenty-four/seven, within the boundary.

"Not withstanding she shall be saved in childbearing if she continues in faith, charity, and holiness with sobriety." (1 Timothy 2:15, KJV)

Women must be aware of the fact that childbearing alone does not save them. The childbearing years help only when attached to the spiritual qualities outlined in the Bible for women. Having these qualities is the only way she will experience the benefits of childbearing. Otherwise, she is just producing offspring. Three of the spiritual qualities needed are of faith, charity, and holiness. Whether she is married, divorced, widowed, or single, she must adhere to Paul's words.

Faith: Faith in God is a form of confidence and this means not being afraid of that which we cannot see with the physical eye nor hear with the natural ears. In faith, the woman must have confidence in God and believe in His Word without having physical proof. She must have faith in the way which God has arranged the order of things. Having faith in God removes the curiosity from the minds of women.

> *"Now, faith is the assurance of things hoped for, the conviction of the things not seen. For by it, people of old received their commendation." (Hebrews 11:1-2, ESV)*

Throughout the Bible, there are several stories of women who had incredible faith in God. Let's consider the faith of Mary, the mother of Jesus. She was by nature like any other woman, curious to have answers to the questions that began to plague her mind. She handled this curiosity with grace and immediately relinquished all these thoughts and gave trust to God (see Luke 1:26-35).

Salome, the mother of the apostles James and John (known as the "Sons of Thunder"), had extraordinary faith in God. She is referred to as the wife of Zebedee. Salome believed in Jesus so that she fell to her knees and asked Him if her sons could sit at His right and left hand in His kingdom. She was part of the group that accompanied Jesus on His final journey from Galilee to Jerusalem (see Matthew 20:20-28 and 27:56).

Charity: In charity, she is in the quality of love. She has, the ability to show and feel affection for others in, spite of a hostile environment. She will show love for her husband, children, and others. Accomplishments of love are shown through sharing with, caring for, and helping others. The help must be done without the attitude of prejudice or hostility.

In other words, she must have the ability to tolerate the different opinions of others without showing unfriendliness or aggressiveness. She may encounter people who are irrational and cannot control their tongue. She must remember to remain in a state of love, especially toward these ones.

> *"A gentle answer deflects anger, but harsh words make tempers flare." (Proverbs 15:1, NLT)*

> *"Beloved, if God so loved us, we ought to love one another. No one has ever seen God; if we love one another, God*

abides in us and his love is perfected in us." (1 John 4:11-12, ESV)

Charity helps to build the tolerance level. Charity helps the woman in that she is able to endure beforehand the things that arouse and stir her emotions. While in this tolerance phase, the woman is showing herself to have spiritual qualities. She is aware of Satan's tactics, ignores her aroused flesh, and continues to trust in God's way of handling things.

> *"Let your speech always be gracious, seasoned with salt, so that you may know how you ought to answer each person."* (Colossians 4:6, ESV)

> *"We make a living by what we get, we make a life by what we give." (Winston Churchill)*

While in charity, we show we are agreeing with the way God has outlined our lives. It also shows the woman is not out of boundary or in opposition to God. Little does she know this is an admirable quality. It sets an example of godliness and decency for all who are listening. Blessing someone using kind conversation is a result of God's grace in our lives. When we are being a blessing to others, this shows we are allowing the order of God's will to be first and foremost in our life.

Holiness: Staying connected with God through His Word and having the spiritual qualities of a woman and displaying them on, a daily basis. The woman is to remain in holiness with sobriety, always, for freedom of the snares by the devil. In holiness, she is always in close association with God. Holiness was God's will and purpose for the nation of Israel. God commanded the Israelites to live holy and sanctified lives separated from Satan.

> *"The Lord God said to Moses, Give the following instructions to the entire community of Israel. You must be holy because I, the Lord your God am holy." (Leviticus 19:1-2, NLT)*

THE LORD COMMENDS OUR EFFORTS

The spiritual quality of holiness in a woman proves that she is in association with God. It also shows an excellent part of her character. In holiness, she is displaying a separation from the sinful patterns of the world. Through a spiritual connection with the Lord, she presents an attitude toward others that is acceptable in the eyes of our Heavenly Father. In maintaining these morals, the woman's emotions are safe from touching the boundary lines. Under God's control, she is safe from the attacks of the enemy.

> *"Therefore, dear brothers and sisters, you have no obligation to do what your sinful nature urges you to do. For if you live by its dictates, you will die. But if through the power of the Spirit you put to death the deeds of your sinful nature, you will live. For all who are led by the Spirit of God are children of God." (Romans 8:12-14, NLT)*

Men and women alike, if we ever find that our spiritual hunger for God is decreasing, we should rethink our priorities. Today, as in past times, sanctification is a requirement for all Christians to follow. In the New Testament of the Bible, holiness is described as a lifelong process by which we continue to put to death our impulses of sin. True holiness requires all believers devote themselves to prayer and participate in fellowship with other Christians. Holiness is needed to live pure and blameless lives, pleasing to our Heavenly Father.

> "Be blessed to live another day."
> "Be thankful for what you have."
> "Time is valuable, spend it wisely."
> "Things happen for a reason."
> "God is always with you."

In coping with adversity, we must put our faith in the Lord and He will help guide us on the path of joy. He provides us with a source of satisfaction and enjoyment while on earth. We must, however, share this great delight by passing it to the next person. Through testimony, verbal communication, prayer, and acts of kindness, the gospel of Jesus Christ travels throughout the world.

> *"For it is not the one who commends himself who is approved, but the one whom the Lord commends." (2 Corinthians 10:18, ESV)*

CHAPTER 10

A DEMEANOR WORTH PERFECTING

"What you notice, give attention to, talk about, get all worked up over emotionally is what you are inviting into your life, whether you mean to or not." (Catherine Ponder)

A composed spirit is without doubt one to acquire; a demeanor which is pleasing to God and others. This demeanor is worth perfecting. A composed spirit is cool and calm, a submissive spirit. True feminine beauty is not the outward appearance of a woman. It is the inner loveliness of a gentle and quiet spirit.

The Apostle Paul brings a certain point to our attention concerning the demeanor of females. He talks about how females are vulnerable and prone to negative influence. This influence comes directly from Satan and shows itself in various forms of attack on God's will and purpose. Yet, the woman can acquire a certain demeanor that diminishes the power of the enemy to control her.

"And no wonder, for even Satan disguises himself as an angel of light." (2 Corinthians 11:14, ESV)

"Let a woman learn quietly with all submissiveness. I do not permit a woman to teach or to exercise authority over a man; rather, she is to remain quiet. For Adam was formed first, then Eve; and Adam was not deceived, but the woman was deceived and became a transgressor." (1 Timothy 2:11-14, ESV)

We should all have the appreciation and concern Paul had for women. His recommendation is the woman should learn in silence. Learning in silence is when the Lord is present. The apostle didn't say a woman is to be quiet at all times. His point is that during quiet times, the Holy Spirit is present, and this allows her to gain special knowledge from God's Word. Quiet times are when there is an absence of Satan's presence; the enemy has no occupied space in the mind. I believe these are the quiet times both apostles speak about.

Quietness is the best time for anyone to learn because the environment is peaceful and without distractions and negative energy. This negativity is from Satan and can block the understanding and hinder spiritual growth. During this time, the knowledge has a chance to penetrate her mind and heart.

Unfortunately, some women are at high risk of attacks from Satan; he can influence with false thoughts that can be perceived as real. Therefore, she is safer while under specific guidelines and restrictions. The negative influence and attacks on her may cause spiritual problems for herself and those around her. Still, God has each woman tucked neatly and safely in His plan. He takes our faithful efforts and multiplies them far beyond what we could imagine or hope for.

- Can women be in a position of leadership in the church congregation?
- Can they serve alongside men in some of the same capacity?
- Can they pray aloud in a group or congregation where men are present?
- Can they serve as biblical teachers where men are present?

The answer to all of these questions is yes. As long as God is receiving the glorification and He is pleased with her actions, she may serve and use her voice to benefit His kingdom. At the same time, the woman must be currently under the spiritual leadership and guidance of a pastor or male leader.

While learning, another good channel for greatness women can use is being under the compelling force of their husbands. This advice from Paul is given because when it comes to spiritual things, God's way is still in its perfect place. The husband must be in close association with God and have influence over his wife's thoughts, interests, and desires. This order is given to help her gain the spiritual knowledge to be appreciated.

As she is loved, cherished, and adored by her husband, she will highly regard his spiritual leadership. She will realize this is a blessing and be grateful for God's way of doing things. Is marriage a command of God? Is marriage recommended for all? What about those who have no spouse? We will elaborate further as we go through this chapter.

IS MARRIAGE A COMMAND OF GOD?

Thousands of years ago, God arranged the spiritual order of things and set up His kingdom in a way that glorifies Him. We can see the importance of each order given to humanity. Nevertheless, we should appreciate God's recommendations and use them as a spiritual guide for our lives.

Marriage is one of the recommendations of God from which some or even most people will benefit. Marriage can give an advantage to our spiritual life because it puts a person in position to develop and maintain godly qualities. It decreases the chances of becoming involved in sexual immoralities.

The Bible's counsel and recommendation on marriage comes directly from God. We have sound advice on ways of conducting our personal life in a way that is pleasing to Him. These recommendations are set in place for you and me to receive the best results of life while here on earth. God has high standards for His people on marriage, cleanliness, and sexuality. We have the best life when we are under God's leadership. We have the best life when we accept His counsel.

> "Let marriage be held in honor among all, and let the marriage bed be undefiled, for God will judge the sexually immoral and adulterous." (Hebrews 13:4, ESV)

> "Marriage is honorable in all and the bed undefiled but whoremongers and adulterers God will judge." (Hebrews 13:4, KJV)

Marriage is worthy of praise in that it is beneficial in many ways. It holds a high reputation for spiritual qualities and recognized by God, the angels, and humans as excellent. There is valid credit given in regard to the manifestation of the glory of God.

One of the ways God is glorified is through marriages. The conduct of two individuals is in agreement and this represents holiness. God is holy. Being one in holy matrimony is an attribute of God and is one of His greatest tools used in the sanctification of mankind. Marriage mirrors God's covenant relationship with His people. God uses implementations to transform followers of Jesus into the image of Him. I make a formal statement saying, "God's will is highly observed and His advice is forever excellent."

Although the desire to be married or remain single is a personal choice, we must keep in mind that the command is "if and when spiritually necessary." God's recommendations put people in line to initiate obedience to Him in many ways. Accepting the recommendation of marriage helps to keep people away from a lifestyle of fornication and adultery. What an excellent way to demonstrate the covenant relationship between Jesus and His bride, the church.

> *"Two are better than one, because they have a good reward for their toil. For if they fall, one will lift up his fellow. But woe to him who is alone when he falls and has not another to lift him up!" (Ecclesiastes 4:9-10, ESV)*

> *"No one who abides in him keeps on sinning; no one who keeps on sinning has either seen him or known him." (1 John 3:6, ESV)*

IS MARRIAGE RECOMMENDED FOR ALL?

The most important relationship we will ever have is with Jesus. On the other hand, one of the most important relationships we will ever have while on earth is with a spouse. However, a person should not enter into marriage expecting their spouse to fulfill their insecurities; these can only be filled by having a relationship with Jesus Christ.

Naturally, we all have issues that we face daily and the majority in part has to do with sin. There are several methods outlined in the Bible to help control these points in question. One method is marriage. It holds spiritual benefits, which include both our physical and spiritual wellbeing.

On the other hand, singles are in no way inferior to married couples in the eyes of God. Single people are not forgotten. They have the same opportunity to gain spiritual honor as married couples. As long as they are abiding in His Word, the Lord reaps tremendous benefits of the work singles put into His kingdom.

When it comes to single Christian women, nothing is more desirable than to have the grace of God provided in everyday life. It's a gracious woman that God blesses, one that is full of joy and expresses her love toward others. Many gracious women are single, divorced, or widowed.

> *"Gracious women have the ability to have and hold honor."*
> *(Proverbs 11:16, KJV)*

The Bible gives an account in 1 Kings 4:1-6 of a widow woman and her two children who were forsaken and desperately needed help. God graciously takes care of them by performing a miracle through Elisha shown in acts of compassion. The Lord was able to use Elisha in this situation because he was a holy man, pure and devoted to the Lord. Because of his faith in God, Elisha was chosen to intervene in a despairing situation.

Being single is not a punishment or curse. It's often assumed in our society that there's something rather odd about you if you're not married. Single Christians have an opportunity to devote themselves more fully to God's work because they have more time to give to such things. Both married and single people are equally important to God. If you have the gift of singleness, that is to exercise self-control, embrace this heavenly blessing. Say, "Thank you Lord Jesus for your power and control over my life."

> *"Now as a concession, not a command, I say this. I wish that all wee as myself am. But each has his own gift from*

> God, one of one kind and one of another. To the unmarried
> and widows, I say that it is good for them to remain single
> as I am. But if they cannot exercise self-control, they should
> marry. For it is better to marry than to burn with passion."
> (1 Corinthians 7:6-9, ESV)

My thirty years of singleness was both grief and an expression of the Lord showing His supernatural powers to me. These years were an opportunity for the Lord to work with me one-on-one, show His greatness, and perform miracles right before my eyes. Although it took me a while to see and realize the depth of God's love for me, His blessings still flowed in my life.

The Lord provide me with a list of promises and most of these promises have come true and some are still playing out right in front of me. As an outcome, single women can also have great opportunity to reap blessings poured out by God if only you trust in Him.

- Don't give up.
- Don't throw in the towel.
- Lift high your palms to God.
- Give Him praise for His everlasting love.
- Thank Him for His provisions.

The Bible is filled with stores of God's blessings and miracles. In the Old and New Testament, He performed amazing results and gave powerful examples of His authority and capabilities. Nothing is impossible for God. Even in singleness, you can always approach Him in confidence knowing that He will hear your prayers. Invite Him to work in every situation in which you are seeking miracles. Pray about any blockages where Satan is preventing these miracles from taking place in your life.

> "What is impossible with man is possible with God." (Luke
> 18:27, NLT)

If one considering marriage, please realize having a spouse does not free you from all the troubles of the flesh. Only a close relationship with the Lord can solve every problem. Although being married has great benefits and an extra spiritual covering for the woman, it does not automatically make the troubles disappear.

Marriage does, however, ease the heavy burdens of life on earth. Many times, these burdens have a negative effect on a person's spiritual stability. These troubles can cause one to sin against God. If marriage is done according to the Word of God, the recommendation to marry is a perfect solution.

TO BE AS THOUGH YOU HAVE NO MATE

When married, Paul reminds the couple there will be trouble in the flesh. He says the troubles of both partners will be spared if they take his advice to be as though they have no mate. How can one be married, nevertheless, and be as though you have no mate? This is a powerful statement from Paul to those considering marriage and for those already married. (See 1 Corinthians 7:25-34.)

Paul is not saying Christians should turn their backs on marriage. Nor is he saying for couples to abandon their marriage vows made under oath in the presence of God. Let's stop and think for a moment. What is Paul saying? He wants us to take into consideration the time is drawing near. The time is limited for doing God's work and Christ's return is nearly approaching. He reminds us that we must not be overly preoccupied with earthly issues and life in this world should not be our highest concern.

A couple cannot attempt to get in this advice line if trust is absent from their marriage. In order to receive Paul's advice, there must be genuine trust between the two. Otherwise, Satan will use this negative energy with effort; he pushes the couple into a well that he has dug. That well is the Divorce Well. Yes, each mate has an obligation to protect each other and watch out for each other's soul. But, having no trust in your mate is not the same as watching out for their soul. Sadly, the one untrusting one is merely watching out for the flesh of self.

The Apostle Matthew records the words of Jesus saying we should not be concerned with this present life but look to the kingdom of God and His righteousness. *"Therefore, I tell you do not be anxious about your* life … But seek first the kingdom of God and his righteousness and all these things will be added to you" (Matthew 6:25, 33, ESV).

To be as though you have no mate, individuals, married or single, must keep their focus solely toward the Lord. There should be a greater degree of focus on pleasing God and He should be the center of their attention. Paul gives this advice because of the human flesh. Trouble can and will arise when there is an extreme degree of attention placed on pleasing one's mate.

In other words, when one mate is seeking a certain degree of attention, this flesh may easily get in a state of dependency. At the same time, one mate may be aggressive and begin to make high demands to be satisfied. Such state of mind increases a craving called selfishness. Other cravings such as jealousy, inconsideration, and grudging are all forms of the flesh seeking gratification.

When contentions arise between couples, it not only affects their relationship with each other, but it affects their personal relationships with Jesus and creates a barrier between their prayers to God. To keep this from happening, each mate must follow the advice given by Paul and understand the things concerning the flesh.

To be as though you have not mate does not mean each partner should deny the other's right to normal satisfaction that are natural and God-given. Failure to fulfill God-given needs in a marriage opens up a can of worms for Satan to use against the marriage, such as adultery. Marriage is emphasized as a lifelong commitment and the presence of the Lord in it signifies a strong bond.

> "Do not deprive each other of sexual relations, unless you both agree to refrain from sexual intimacy for a limited time so you can give yourselves more completely to prayer. Afterward, you should come together again so that Satan won't be able to tempt you because of your lack of self-control." (1 Corinthians 7:5, NLT)

When Christians act as though they have no mate, including singles, they are caring for the things of the Lord. Full focus of godly things is the most important way for all of us to offer undivided attention to serving the Lord. The theme of the Apostle Paul is the focus of our heart and mind should be absolutely on the kingdom of God.

If Christians are married, the best part of being as though you have no mate is that the marriage automatically receives blessings from the Lord. Putting the Lord first in everything and ignoring the nagging flesh, marriage will survive the difficult times.

Remember the words of Paul in 1 Corinthians 7:29-34. He said, "*The time is short. From now on, those who have wives should live as though they have none. And this I speak for your own profit; not that I may cast a snare on you, but for that which is comely, and to always be sure to attend upon the Lord without distraction.*"

When remembering the fact of little time left on earth, there is not a waste in precious moments trying to satisfy the flesh. The flesh cannot be completely satisfied or permanently gratified. While keeping our minds and hearts upon the Lord, there will be no undue fleshly fulfillments. Whether married or single, the focus is solely on satisfying the Lord and fulfilling the will of God without distractions.

Anything or anyone that captures my attention and causes me to lose focus of the kingdom is considered a distraction. For example, when driving a car, one must remain focused and not allow distractions to move their mind away from the road. A bird minding its flying business, or children in the backseat crying for attention, divides our attention. No matter how loud the baby cries, the driver must remain in a certain frame of mind in order to maintain control of the vehicle, then safely pull off the road and give attention to the baby.

> "*I am saying this for your benefit, not to place restrictions on you. I want you to do whatever will help you serve the Lord best, with as few distractions as possible.*" (1 Corinthians 7:35, NLT)

In the kingdom of God, certain demands for attention can be a distraction, drawing one's devotion away from the zealously serving the Lord. When being as though we have no mate, we must maintain control of our thoughts, actions, and reactions. We must not allow certain activity to interfere, which can cause destruction.

The driver of the car may have to act as though there are no birds flying or children crying in order to maintain control. Likewise, each one of us may have to be as though we have no mate for the sake of maintaining spiritual focus. The attention is solely upon the Lord. We can do this seemingly hard but simple task by ignoring the nagging flesh. Let's all keep in mind the importance of heavenly things that set us apart from the world.

> *"In all thy ways acknowledge him, and he shall direct thy paths." (Proverbs 3:6, KJV)*

— CHAPTER 11 —

SEDUCING SPIRITS

"For the message of the cross is foolishness to those who are perishing, but to us who are being saved it is the power of God." (1 Corinthians 1:18, NIV)

On the other hand of God's proposal given to mankind, several may possibly benefit from marriage but refuse the Bible's recommendations given. The Apostle Paul expresses his concerns of this very thing happening on earth during the latter 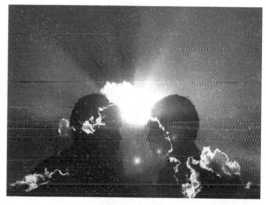 times which we are living in. During the last days, there will be evil spirits that will seduce people into being insubordinate to God.

These evil spirits are so clever in that they will have some people forbidding marrying. The spirits influence the minds of people not to get married even when marriage is best for that person; thus, giving them an opportunity to succeed spiritually. Their drive to generate disobedience in God affects both men and women.

The deceitful spirits Paul talks about in 1 Timothy are evil spirits. They seduce the minds of some people and lead them into wrong decisions through influence. These evil spirits manipulate people into being insubordinate to God. They compel some of the people not to accept the advice of our Lord—in particular, his recommendation on marriage.

Paul explains that the Spirit of God speaks about this in an expressive way. In other words, God's spirit makes an exact statement about the seducing spirits and the doctrine of devils. He clearly states we must have a transparent understanding of the apostasy, which is the desertion of moral principles.

> "Now the Spirit expressly says that in latter times some will depart from the faith by devoting themselves to deceitful spirits and teachings of demons, through the insincerity of liars whose consciences are seared, who forbid marriage and require abstinence from foods that God created to be received with thanksgiving by those who believe and know the truth. For everything God created is good." (1 Timothy 4:1-4a, ESV)

> *"I am afraid that as the serpent deceived Eve by his cunning, your thoughts will be led astray from a sincere and pure devotion to Christ." (2 Corinthians 11:3, ESV)*

Satan, in the form of an evil spirit, tried influencing Jesus. *"The devil took him to a very high mountain and showed him all the kingdoms of the world and their glory" (Matthew 4:8, ESV).*

We must be absolutely, certain whether our decision to marry or remain single is the will of God for us. When we fail to accept the recommendation and advice of God, we are doing a disservice to our own spiritual life. Therefore, ignoring God's counsel puts us in vulnerable positions to be attacked by the seducing spirits. A precious life turns out to be the opposite of God's will for that person. The possibility is great for becoming involved with fornication, adultery, and other illicit acts that are not pleasing to God.

The Apostle John also talks about the seducing spirits doing their works of deceit. He mentions the Antichrist is one of the seducing spirits that influences the minds of people to go against Christ. He is speaking passionately about the seducing spirits and out of concern for us, he wants God's people to be aware of their influence. We must be in tune with the reality of these evil spirits and how they operate.

> "Children, it is the last hour, and as you have heard that the antichrist is coming, so now many antichrists have come. Therefore, we know that it is the last hour." (1 John 2:18, ESV)

> "These things in which he has written down are concerning them that seduce you." (1 John 2:26, KJV)

> "The coming of the lawless one is by the activity of Satan with all power and false signs and wonders, and with all wicked deception for those who are perishing, because they refused to love the truth and so be saved." (2 Thessalonians 2:9-10, ESV)

In Revelation, John also explains the words he heard from the Son of Man were words concerning the seducing spirits. He tells us the Son of Man speaks to the fourth angel and said:

> "I know your works, your love and faith and service and patient endurance, and that your latter works exceed the first. But I have this against you, that you tolerate that woman Jezebel, who calls herself a prophetess and is teaching and seducing my servants to practice sexual immorality and to eat food sacrificed to idols." (Revelation 2:19-20, NLT)

During our current times, a seduction process is taking place. The seducing spirits are influencing the nations to commit fornication, adultery, and other illicit acts of immorality. People of all cultures, ages, nationality, and religion are at risk. Many people refuse to marry when they are involved in such acts. Having sexual intercourse outside of marriage is fornication and/or adultery; this is against the will of God.

The spirit of Jezebel is another controlling evil spirit that is alive and affecting the minds of many to the point that they refuse to acknowledge a mere stated fact: they should marry. This spirit's main objective is to influence the mentality of people to manipulate and dominate everything and everyone. Those under this spirit refuse to accept God's will and they are not willing to give of themselves and consent to marriage.

BENEFITS OF THE RECOMMENDATION

Our souls crave intimacy, and marriage is earth's most intimate communion between humans. Marriage can provide a spiritual refuge and sanctuary for some. Taking the relationship from commitment to a place of peace can be heavenly, a gift from God. The first marriage took place between a man and a woman in the Garden of Eden. Marriage is not just a mere contract between two people; it is a way of life that offers continual loving service to the one with whom you have chosen to spend the rest of your life.

The course of action given to marriage has great benefits. There is respect given for your mate's space and attention given to small impressions. Each still has the opportunity, nevertheless, to express moments of solitude and find refuge in the presence of God. When two people marry, they become one, sharing a life where there are both happy and sad moments. Marriage is the greatest support system life on earth has to offer. Having someone to give you the strength and determination needed to become a better person is an anchor to keep you grounded.

Following the Bible's advice on marriage, we can be free of the controlling spirits that seduces people to go against the righteousness of God. A method that helps to avoid in fornication and adultery and other immoral acts against God.

> *"From the beginning of creation, God make them male and female. Therefore, a man shall leave his father and mother and hold fast to his wife, and the two shall become one flesh. So, they are no longer two but one flesh. What therefore God has joined together, let not man separate."* (Mark 10:6-9, NLT)

The Bible also gives advice to widows, divorced women, and young women. If they are unable to contain themselves, which includes being in control of the emotional issues they faced daily, it is better for them to marry. Females are sensitive to many things and for some, it may mean being easily influenced and provoked into doing and saying wicked things. God wants His people to be holy and blameless. He wants us to avoid anything that is not morally pure.

> *"I would have younger widows marry, bear children, manage their households, and give the adversary no occasion for slander." (1 Timothy 5:14, ESV)*

This spiritual place of refuge shelters from the dangers and it also minimizes the distress of handling personal issues on our own. When a woman has the protection of her husband, he offers her an opportunity to rest. Marriage can provide an opportunity to be free from the influence of Satan's manipulation. There is less chance she will be Satan's target.

Marriage may perhaps lessen the chance of an attack because the husband is in direct control of her interests and providing spiritual protection. At the same time, her mind is busy concentrating on providing care to her family, which leaves less room for Satan to hassle her and plant evil and negative thoughts.

While the wife is submitting to her husband in the Lord, this makes it easy for the husband to use his God-given ability to provide special protection for himself, his wife, and family. The husband can help his wife deal with her shortcomings. He can assist her in finding her position of godliness where she is not a target of Satan. Accepting the advice of Paul shows they are both in agreement with the recommendations of God.

INSUBORDINATE WOMAN/WIFE

This subject is often shunned because no one wants to offend the woman. We as women shall not be contingent because we always rely on what the Bible has to say. Did God create man and woman as equal? Entirely so. Both are responsible and accountable to God on an equal stand. This equality does not mean physically because they are biologically different in many ways. What makes them equal is they both bear the same image of God and He loves them both the same.

However, their roles on earth are different and these roles are first mentioned in the book of Genesis. Yes, men and women are created equally but they don't always have the same roles. According to Genesis 3, because of sin, it is a woman's impulse that has them to try to rule over her husband. During the punishment phase of Adam and Eve's disobedience, God chose man to be the provider and protector and the woman as comforter and nurturer.

God says to Eve, *"I will sharpen the pain of your pregnancy, and in pain you will give birth. Your desire will be for your husband, and he will rule over you"* (Genesis 3:16 NLT).

God says to Adam, *"Because you listened to your wife and ate fruit from the tree about which I commanded you, 'You must not eat from it, cursed is the ground because of you'"* (Genesis 3:16-17a, NLT).

In order for a married woman to have spiritual success and gain the full benefits of life, she must always remain in a position of submission to her husband and/or other spiritual leaders, rather than seeking to control. In this position, she accepts and respects the authority of the male's role and their leadership over her.

On the other hand, if she is not married, she is under the same obligation to stand in a submissive location as a godly woman. Marriage may or may not be the best for her, but each decision she makes must be tracked through the same spiritual package holding the same guidelines and regulations. The Lord watches over each, and every woman the same.

> *"I will instruct you and teach you in the way you should go; I will counsel you with my eye upon you."* (Psalm 32:8, ESV)

In either case, married or single, for the sake of her soul each woman must follow God's word and fully accept the spiritual assistance provided to her. Eliminating portions of the Word of God gives birth to unpleasant traits, which simply manifest itself through rebellion. The Proverbs mention one trait in particular: the odious behavior of a woman. This behavior is disgraceful and born out of wickedness, a demeanor proving that there is a lack of submission to God.

> *"For three things, the earth is disquieted, and four which it cannot bear: For a servant when he reigneth; and a fool*

*when he is filled with meat; For an odious woman when
she is married; and a handmaid that is heir to her mistress."
(Proverbs 30:21-23, KJV)*

An odious woman is factually under the attack of a seducing spirit belonging to Satan. She may be married or single, with or without children. She is one who is not in control of her emotional issues. Her ungodly desires cause displeasure to those in her midst. She is expressing this contempt because she wants her way. An odious woman displays this character in various forms of words, gestures, and impressions.

If this woman is married, her husband is embarrassed by the behavior and if single others are offended by the lack of compassion. She shows dislike and disgust for things that are not on a personal approval list. Unfortunately, the attitude is often hidden beneath the surface and not easily interpreted.

Whether married or single, the spirit-seduced woman collectively pushes her behavior toward a disgrace to society. If she does not listen to the spiritual counsel of her leaders, from whom will she accept guidance and discipline? Sadly, more than likely, she will listen to no one. Sadly, the attacks on others are deplorable and continue because she is neither satisfied nor pleased in her own personal pleasures.

Paul speaks about some of the younger widows:

*"They get into the habit of being idle and going about from
house to house. And not only do they become idles, but also
busy bodies who talk nonsense, saying things they ought not
to. So, I counsel younger widows to marry, to have children,
to manage their homes and to give the enemy no opportunity
for slander. Some have in fact already turned away to follow
Satan." (1 Timothy 5:14-15 NIV)*

These words from Paul can be referred to any woman who is idle in her mind and deeds. Words, gestures, and cruel impressions continue to move across the land. Through her selfishness, jealousy, anger, busybody, gossiping, tattling, scheming, envying, and chaos, she spreads it throughout the earth like wildfire.

Regrettable, a domino effect takes place with the other females as they fall prey to the negative energy. Now there is company added to misery and it fuels to the fire. These habits are just as humiliating as the female employee who inherits fortunes from her mystery lover, filled with disgust and offensive to God.

This situation is sad, especially when she is married because the spiritual guidance is there, but she remains under the attack of evilness. A married woman caught-up in an odious attitude does not necessarily mean her husband is not close to God. In addition, it does not mean her husband is not providing for her spiritually. However, it does mean this case, needs extra coverage. A case of this sort must seek additional strength, perhaps from other qualified spiritual leaders.

It is highly probable that this woman maybe in a dire state and not reaping the benefits from the marriage or spiritual counsel and leaders. For one reason or another, she may well be a direct target of the devil and receiving personal attacks from Satan himself.

As a result, she may be in desperate need of spiritual control and authority of God through Jesus Christ. Through fasting and prayer, the Spirit of God breaks through within the soul and allows her to manifest a godly nature. Whether she is married or single, she can survive the attacks of evil and be free of all accusations against her.

There was a case involving relief of Satan's control and it's recorded in the Bible's book of Matthew. The disciples of Jesus were not able to cast out a certain demon that was strong and stubborn. Jesus told His disciples that there are kinds that leave only by way of fasting and prayer.

> *"Jesus rebuked the devil; and he departed out of him: and the child was cured from that very hour. Then came the disciples to Jesus apart, and said, 'Why could not we cast him out?' And Jesus said unto them, "Howbeit this kind goes not out but by prayer and fasting." (Matthew 17:18-21, KJV)*

> *"Afterwards, when Jesus was alone in the house with his disciples, they asked him, 'Why couldn't we cast out that evil spirit?' Jesus replied, 'This kind can be cast out only by prayer.'" (Mark 9:28-29, NLT)*

Upon accepting the spiritual protection and physical limitation, the woman previously distressed may return to her original position, initially set by God. The same position designed to cover her with elegance and grace—submission to God. This position of submission:

- benefits her spiritually, physically, and emotionally
- helps the woman gain spiritual qualities
- allows her to have an advantage over her emotional outbursts
- helps to overcome extreme distresses, which cause the outbursts
- gives her the opportunity to express love openly
- teaches her to be supportive to her husband, family, and others
- gives her a favorable chance to gain an excellent degree of her nature as a godly woman.

Whether a woman has a displeasing nature to God, or she is simply immature, she may require an intervention from the Lord: a special overseer from God to help neutralize her nature. This point stems around the Garden of Eden. Mediating on this thought and thinking of Eve, I often wondered if she was the odious type, inattentive, or a bit naïve when Satan proposed the lie to her that would affect every woman after her.

No matter the case of Eve, the Lord still blessed her by providing the necessary spiritual coverage that helped her to gain everlasting life in the presence of God. Eve lived out the rest of her natural life on earth covered with grace. The Bible informs us of her regrets and her rejoices. We can acquire knowledge from Eve's life while she was on earth.

Many women look in the mirror and pay close attention to themselves. In this clear picture, can you see yourself in the Garden of Eden surrounded by the beautiful flowers and the smell of cleanness? Do you desire to be content, but then realize you're vulnerable and exposed to danger? If so, asks the Lord this question: "Lord, according to your will, what is best for me and my life?"

> "When I look at your heavens, the work of your fingers, the moon and the stars, which you have set in place, what is man that you are mindful of him, and the son of man that you care for him?" (Psalm 8:3-4, ESV)

> The Lord said, *"If anyone would come after me, let him deny himself and take up his cross daily and follow me"* (*Luke 9:23, ESV*).

For this vulnerable creature standing in the mirror examining her life, a special man of God, may be needed to assist in building a wall against the enemy. This is a peculiar type of man and he has a unique character. He is able to stand in the gap because he is so close to God. He is also inaccessible to Satan, this evil one does not stand a chance with him. Nothing can pry him loose from the love he has for his Lord and Savior—not even his wife.

At times, this man of God may appear stubborn and inflexible to her wants and desires, but this man is walking directly in the honor of God's Holy Spirit. He stays in close association with God, and all things in life he does and says are according to the will of God. He is confident in his walk with Jesus and has a positive influence on those around him.

Proverbs mentions this peculiar and faithful man of God: *"Many a man proclaims his own steadfast love, but a faithful man who can find?"* (*Proverbs 20:6-7, ESV*)

For the woman, whose married to this special man her chance of spiritual survival is greater because her husband is mainly interested in pleasing God. As she humbly submits herself to her husband and his servant's leadership, she is automatically safe and free from the attacks of the evil one. Her prayer is:

> O Lord, I thank you for revealing my complete plan through your Word, thank you that I am delivered from the insubordinate spirit. Help me to become the woman who quickly chooses humility. Give me the quality of being discreet. Let the heart of my husband trust me completely. Have me to do him good all the days of my life. Allow me to see the glory of thy lasting joy, holy, holy, holy are you, everlasting Lord. Amen!

— CHAPTER 12 —

SUPERNATURAL EFFECT

Some may call it a bad omen, but it's negative energy that can wreak havoc on an innocent life. This energy comes from the master of evil and can rock or ruin a seemingly perfect individual, family, or structure. When this energy is present, the destruction it causes is sometimes discussed for years because of its effect.

A few years ago, a man I'll call Lucas had it all together: a wonderful life with a wife and kids, a great job, and a nice house. Because of his bubbly personality, all those who, came in contact with him loved him. He was offered great opportunity for prosperity and success. The blessings from God bestowed upon Lucas showered an effect every American would dream of.

Unfortunately, Lucas opened himself up to sin and stepped out of boundary. His definition of happiness began to change when he developed in his heart an attraction to illicit drugs. This attraction was bigger than life itself. Despite problems it posed on him and his family, he spent every penny he had on this unhealthy lifestyle. He had become bound by the law of sin and death and his spiritual status with God became an illusion. The reality of it as his loved ones and friends knew, Lucas was lost.

There were many who reached out to help, including the doctors and professional counselors at the rehab centers. In, spite of this help and prayers going up on his behalf, Lucas still couldn't seem to find his way home because the enemy of God had control of him. To no avail, the infliction remained and this predicament in Lucas' life took a toll on him and cost him a close relationship with God. Like so many others with similar issues, Lucas lost it all: his family, a secure job, and sadly, the respect from those he loved.

Lucas needed a supernatural cleansing from God, one that would restore him not only physically, but also spiritually. The master of evil wreaked havoc on his life and he needed a restoral. A new and tender heart is a receptive heart—one that would have had Lucas to respond to God's Word. Lucas never got a chance to have a meaningful and successful life again because, he died before that opportunity arose.

> *"I will sprinkle clean water on you and you will be clean; I will cleanse you from all your impurities and from all your idols." (Ezekiel 36:25, NIV)*

> *"Every good and perfect gift is from above, coming down from the Father of the heavenly lights, who does not change like the shifting shadows." (James 1:17, NIV)*

When the spiritual line has been crossed, this puts one in direct territory of Satan. This is a foul area; therefore, it is forbidden and off limits to God's children. These limitations are for our own safety. Being out of boundary of God's will is being in the realm that belongs to Satan. This is being in the midst of evil. It's a dangerous place to be since it belongs to Satan and is controlled by him and his demons.

The environmental conditions of this area are cut off from the association of God. There is sound evidence that this area is where chaotic conditions are born and arise to heights beyond our own ability to repair. Being in the midst of evil certainly blocks us from having a close relationship with our Lord and Savior, Jesus Christ.

Excessive attractions and extreme reactions are signs that a person's character maybe out of boundary and in need of an adjustment. This is one time to repent and request a makeover from God through prayer. These signs are clear evidence that this individual has issues pertaining to the heart and the Lord is the only one who can cleanse our heart for us. The Lord is holy and the only one who can exchange our weaknesses for joy.

> *"Repent then and turn to God, so that your sins may be*
> *wiped out, that times of refreshing may come from the Lord,*
> *and that he may send the Messiah, who has been appointed*
> *for you – even Jesus." (Acts 3:19-20, NIV)*

Honesty to God about our defective character and sincerity in our devotion to please Him is the first step in gaining a spiritual cleansing. Coupled with prayer a recovery process begins to take place. Acquiring a righteous lifestyle, one can begin to reflect on what is right by God's standards. Since the issues in question are mostly pertaining to the heart, the cleansing may not be quick and easy.

An indisputable fact is one must not be in denial of the truth about possibly being stuck across the boundary line. Our confession of violating morals and principles is none other than support to a successful recovery. Paying attention to our attitude, motives, and recognizing certain behaviors are sure ways we can begin this spiritual recovery.

King David was a person who knew God and he had keen pleasure of spiritual salvation. He was placed by God in position of power over the people of Israel. He was given an anointing to use for the purpose of magnifying the power of God. There was a time when David took advantage of this power because his flesh had taken control over what he knew was right. He disrespected God by stepping out of line.

In misuse of God's power, David treated the Word of God with disdain. He ultimately came under great conviction and suffered the consequences of his actions. The book of Psalms shows David's repentance as he prays to God for forgiveness. He asked the Lord to cleanse his heart of his evil ways and wrongdoings. He also asked God to renew his spirit, which means he wanted his spirit to be changed.

There was evidence that David needed a heart cleansing and renewed spirit because of the ungodly things he was involved in. When he paid attention to behaviors and recognized that his character was not pleasing to God, he confessed his sins. His affair with Bathsheba, the death of Bathsheba's husband Uriah, and the death of his own son were a transparency of his sin. David was overwhelmed with feelings of guilt, so he called upon the Lord in his troubles and he asked for help.

If we have in any way disrespected God's Word or His power, we can likewise follow David's example and request a spiritual cleansing from God. A purging takes place as our soul is washed clean by God. We then live our life in ways that will teach others about the love and grace of God. Here is a prayer modeled after David's prayer of forgiveness.

> A PRAYER FOR SPIRITUAL CLEANSING
> (*Example prayer is taken from Psalm 51:1-15, KJV*)
> *"Dear Father, Hear my prayer. Oh God, please have mercy upon me according to your loving kindness. Give ear to the words of my mouth.*
> *Today, I acknowledge I have sinned against you by being in, the midst of evil conditions and situations.*
> *Purge me with hyssop, cleanse me of all undesirable traits so that I may be white as snow.*
> *Please, create in me a clean heart, renew a right spirit within me so that my behavior may be righteously pleasing to you. Continue to construct my spirit daily into perfect righteousness. I will teach your ways to others who have also gone beyond the boundary line set by you.*
> *I pray these many things in your Son Christ Jesus' name, Amen."*

FAITH IN GOD'S ABILITY TO RETRIEVE US

Nebuchadnezzar was king of the Babylonian Empire from 605 BC to 562 BC. He was the greatest and most powerful of all the kings in Babylon. The Babylonians were heathens and they worshipped Pagan gods who were images. They did not believe in the God of Israel, the creator of heaven and earth. Nebuchadnezzar expected his people to bow to his Pagan gods. In the Bible, Daniel 3 tells the story of three of Daniel's Jewish friends who had to choose between bowing to Nebuchadnezzar's gods or being thrown in a fiery furnace.

The three were Shadrach, Meshach, and Abednego, servants of the true God of Israel. They chose not to bow down to the golden statue because they served the God of Israel, and they would remain faithful to Him no matter what. They maintained their obedience to Him by not bowing to graven images. Nebuchadnezzar was furious and overflowing with rage because they would not serve his statue-made gods. The king immediately ordered them bound and thrown into the deadly inferno. He believed in his heart that no god could save those three from his judgment.

Because of the faithfulness of Shadrach, Meshach, and Abednego, the holy one of Israel preserved them from harm. After they were thrown into the furnace, the king looked and saw four figures, not three, walking unharmed in the inferno flames. Seeing they were unharmed, Nebuchadnezzar knew they were servants of the Most High God.

The king brought them out of the furnace and promoted them to a higher office in the empire. He made a decree that if anyone spoke against the God of Israel, they should be torn, limb from limb. The king saw God's ability to save His people from the hands of any power against Him. *(See Daniel 3:1-30.)*

"There is a river whose streams make glad the city of our God, the holy place where the Most High dwells." (Psalm 46:4, NIV)

Our Father in Heaven is our refuge and strength. He is sovereign over nature and the nations. He always answers our prayers in regard to the desire we have for His presence. When the righteous cry, the Lord hears and delivers them out of all their troubles.

Faith in God and belief our prayer will be answered are keys to turning a difficult situation around. A countless number of times, the Bible gives proof of God's existence and His ability to do the impossible. His timing is perfect; an important part of his plan for humanity and it works hand in hand with our willingness to cooperate.

"Be still before the Lord and wait patiently for him; do not fret when people succeed in their ways, when they carry out their wicked schemes." (Psalm 37:7, NIV)

Taking road trips to Missouri during the summertime were always fun. We looked forward to getting out of school for the summer and spending quality time with family. This was the main subject of discussion during the winter school days. The end of May came and with school report cards received, we looked at the next grade level on the back of the cards and jumped with joy.

Back in the days when seat belts were not an issue, it was 1965 and twelve of us piled into my dad's 1954 station wagon. Along with our sandwiches, fruit, and luggage we headed from Monroe, Louisiana to St. Louis. With the windows rolled down, we could feel the breeze of the summer air. The speed limit back then was fifty-five. Depending on the bathroom breaks and dad needing to rest, the trip took about twelve hours on Interstate 55 to reach our destination.

The city with the large zoo of fascinating animals greeted us with smiles. My dad's cousin and his wife anxiously awaited on their porch with hospitality for us to arrive. Our enjoyable two-week vacation began with hugs and kisses. Then we would run upstairs to claim our sleeping spots. The vacations in St. Louis were always as if it were the first and were a delightful amazement.

On a sunny afternoon, the whole family was at the zoo. Mom pushed my two-year-old brother in the stroller. We stopped at every section where the animals were enclosed by a fence. The monkeys jumped from tree to tree and the gorillas paid close attention to the crowds. They were all such large and beautiful animals. It was getting hot, so Mom decided to take a break. So, she stopped the stroller right in front of the giraffes, who were near the fence. You could reach out and touch their long legs.

Amazed by what he saw, my toddler brother took a long look at the giraffe closest to the fence. He started at the giraffe's feet and slowly worked his way upward until he reached the animal's face. By this time, he tumbled backwards, and the stroller hit the ground. The fall didn't so much as even faze him. He looked into the eyes of this large animal with a big smile on his face. This part of the trip we still laugh about today.

The trip home from St. Louis this summer was still fresh in the mind of my father, Louis Harris right before he passed away of lung cancer. At the time of this writing, he was eighty-two-years-old and still reminiscing of this story, as if it happened yesterday. He always mentioned he would never forget how the Lord showed His power and strength to him. As we drove along the two-lane road of Interstate 55, the sun had gone down, it had just begun to get dark. The singing and counting of cows had ended. All the children had fallen asleep, including my dad's aunt Mira.

Dad and Mom still talked for miles when my mother finally succumbed to her tiredness and fell asleep, too. Being the only driver of the car, my dad drove down the dark highway in silence for hundreds of miles. As he drove by the trees and dark pastures, he did his usual whistling while driving. He realized the entire world was asleep.

In this story, Dad goes on to tell us he must have drifted off to sleep when he heard one of my brothers loudly calling his name. "Dad!" Dad instantly became alert and the last thing he remembered is veering toward the headlights of an eighteen-wheeler. At that moment, he thought we would all probably die. He said he doesn't know how the car ended up back on the proper side of the road, but it did.

The Lord had intervened on behalf of my family and saved our lives. Dad regained control of the vehicle and drove on down the interstate. He immediately realized my brother is asleep.

He called out my brother's name, awakening him, and asked, "What did you want?"

My brother said, "I didn't call you."

My father said he believed an angel of God intervened and spared our lives that night. My dad was forever in awe of how quickly God can move and come to our rescue. This is what I call a supernatural effect.

The power of God Almighty in the heavens can redeem any of us and recover the souls of all those in need of help. We are reminded through the prophet Isaiah this is the same God who delivered Israel from the captivity of Babylon and their gods. He is the same God who dried up the sea, made the rivers into wilderness, and used sackcloth to clothe the heavens with blackness. This is the same God who frees all of us from the hands of Satan.

Our confidence in God may sometimes fail during different experiences but, seeking His face will restore our belief in His powers. At a time of Israel's unfaithfulness, God reinforced Isaiah's confidence in His compassion and strength.

"Was it not you who dried up the sea, the waters of the great deep, who made a road in the depths of the sea so that the redeemed might cross over?" (Isaiah 51:10, NIV)

"He turned rivers into a desert, flowing springs into thirsty ground." (Psalm 107:33, NIV)

"I clothe the heavens with darkness and make sackcloth its covering." (Isaiah 50:3, NIV)

We have an obligation to follow instructions outlined in God's Word. His Word includes His concern for our safety and us being near the face of evil. This information comes directly from God in the form of commands, advice, and suggestions. It puts truth seekers in line to receive a supernatural response when needed. Following these basic steps will keep us on the road to spiritual success. All the information received should be placed in our heart and mind for the sake of our soul.

— CHAPTER 13 —

BIBLICAL LEADERSHIP

*"Remember your leaders, those who spoke to you the word
of God. Consider the outcome of their way of life, and
imitate their faith." (Hebrews 13:7, ESV)*

In the United States, every four years a new leader is sworn into the
highest office achievable, President of the United States of America.
Unless he's voted to a second term, there is a new leader sitting in the
Oval Office, making major decisions for our country. He is one of the
world's most powerful figures and his role includes being commander in
chief of the world's most expensive military. He has the power to declare
war and is held responsible for the protection of the American people.

The President is the head of the executive branch of the federal
government and is constitutionally obligated to take care that the laws
be faithfully executed. He has the power to fire executive officials, which
has been a contentious political issue. Generally, a president may use his
power to remove purely executive officials at will.

However, Congress can curtail and constrain a president's authority
to fire commissioners of independent regulatory agencies and certain
inferior executive officers by statue. The President has the power to
nominate federal judges, including members of the United States Court
of Appeals and the Supreme Court of the United States.

We should always be in prayer for our president; pray that he has a
listening ear for God and he allows the Holy Spirit to guide him as he
directs our country.

When it comes to human leadership, there are many different
definitions throughout the world. The Merriam-Webster Dictionary

in the United States describes leadership as "the power or ability to lead other people" and others say leadership is "the ability to influence production." However, the largest financial education website in the world, Investopedia, describes leadership as "the ability of company's management to set and achieve challenging goals, take swift and decisive actions, outperform the competition, and inspire others to perform well."

While meanings may vary, there is one definition that will always remain the same: spiritual leadership. A spiritual leader is "one that aims to achieve a goal of everlasting life and inspires others along the way." Jesus Christ has the highest spiritual position achievable and His role is to shepherd the people of God and control His kingdom. The value of His leadership is flawless, and it brings about a change to the world.

> *"The Father loves the Son and has placed everything in his hands." (John 3:35, NIV)*

The Bible records the role of leaders with responsibilities similar to that of Christ. Spiritual leaders are possessed by the Holy Spirit with the gift of leadership. Like Jesus, they provide spiritual guidance and methods for us to experience that which is holy and sacred.

Almighty God is sovereign, and He is holy. His ways are pure, and He is highly regarded with reverence; consequently, being in His presence is something sacred. The supreme greatness of His majestic presence is stunning because it's something we don't see among mere humans. God is awesome and all-powerful; His love endures forever.

> *"Tremble, earth, at the presence of the Lord, at the presence of the God of Jacob, who turned the rock into a pool, the hard rock into springs of water." (Psalm 7-8, NIV)*

When that which is spiritual, the Holy Spirit, guides us, we come to an elevated rank of holiness and soar to a place of awe that is the presence of Almighty God. In approaching the presence of God, we must enter His gates with praise and thanksgiving. Oh! What a joyous place to be, no other than in His heavenly domain.

> *"Know that the Lord is God. It is he who made us, and we are his, we are his people, the sheep of his pasture. Enter his gates with thanksgiving and his courts with praise; give thanks to him and praise his name." (Psalm 100:2-4, NIV)*

> *"You have made known to me the paths of life, you will fill me with joy in your presence." (Acts 2:28, NIV)*

Spiritual leadership consists of humility and putting others ahead of you. Jesus Christ gave an example when He humbled Himself to His disciples as the lowest of servants. The day had come for the Jews to celebrate the Passover with a meal. This would be the Last Supper for Jesus with His disciples. He performed a washing of the disciples' feet, which would signify they were spiritually clean and belong to Him.

Jesus knew His hour had come for Him to depart from this world, returning to His Father. He wanted the disciples to understand true greatness comes from serving others. The disciples didn't know the hour had come, but the lesson they would learn on humility continued to be talked about after Jesus died on the cross and returned to His Father. This conversation of how to show courteousness and respect to others will continue until Jesus returns to earth again at the last day.

> *"It was just before the Passover Festival. Jesus knew that the hour had come for him to leave this world and go to the Father. Having loved his own who were in the world, he loved them to the end." (John 13:1, NIV)*

Jesus' disciples didn't understand why He (Jesus), being their master, would be washing their feet. They didn't understand He was on His way to the cross. They didn't know the devil had planted deceit into the heart of a fellow disciple who was about to betray Him. As the Scriptures were being fulfilled, Jesus knew which one of them was filled with evil. He knew which one of the disciples was about to betray him.

He explains to His disciples that they may not understand the washing of the feet now, but they will later. He wanted them to follow this same washing example. Over the next few days, the disciples witnessed the betrayal of Jesus, the tormenting death Jesus endured, and also, His resurrection. They saw the power of God at work gloriously fulfilling Scriptures right before their eyes. *(See John 13:2-17.)*

All the disciples of Jesus except one, Judas Iscariot, supported Him in everything he did while on Earth. Many of His disciples left their family and careers to give assistance to His ministry. They also supported the ministry after Jesus had left the earth and gone back to His Father. The disciples traveled to distant countries, preaching the good news of Christ and His resurrection.

For the sake of their leader, Jesus, those that followed Him were willing to be beaten, imprisoned, and some were even tortured to death. If you were a disciple of Jesus two thousand years ago, would you have supported Him in the same? Today, how do you think you can give support to your spiritual leader or leaders?

> *"Remember your leaders, who spoke the word of God to you. Consider the outcome of their way of life and imitate their faith." (Hebrews 13:7, NIV)*

Two women shared stories on CNN recounting horrific memories of being forced to perform oral sodomy and other sexual acts to a serial rapist with a badge. An Oklahoma City police officer is convicted and gets 263 years in prison for rape, sodomy, and other charges. The twenty-nine-year-old ex-cop and former college football star received a sentence two and a half centuries long. There were over a dozen victims, all women ranging from a seventeen-year-old teenager to a fifty-seven-year-old grandmother of twelve.

Prosecutors said his ruthless scheme began during a June 2014 traffic stop. He was fired from the force in January 2015 after an internal investigation. According to CNN affiliate KFOR, the Oklahoma City Police Chief wrote in the termination letter, "Your offenses committed against women in our community constitute the greatest abuse of police authority I have witnessed in my thirty-seven years as a member of this agency."

This ex-officer had been sworn to an oath and given the power to uphold the law of the land. Instead, he used his badge while on duty to defile his victims. His job was to protect and serve the people in the community, but he became inflated with pride, his oath went out the window, and his flesh got the best of him. This is a sad case of one losing control of his sexual urges. This guy needed a direct intervention of the Lord's hand upon him.

Some people say, "This was not a police officer who committed rape but, a serial rapist masqueraded as a law enforcement officer." He used his badge in a way that smeared a substance of deceit over the eyes of the women he violated.

Today, similar things such as sexual immorality happen in some churches. There are some with authority in the house of the Lord who take advantage of their position and power, using it for their gain and satisfaction. Such leaders are in need of an intervention from the power of God to unlock the leash Satan has on them. Whatever their reasons for mishandling authority, God Himself will not waver. He will handle this type of disrespect against His kingdom.

Some of the women scoped out by such oppression may be weak and complacent, carelessly content and not aware of such schemes. Some may also be naïve and vulnerable to such sinfulness. Others are willing participants of such church scandals because they are satisfied with their current situation and unconcerned with it changing. With their spirituality on the rocks, they continue with life the way it is. These type women stand a high chance to being exposed in the same way Bathsheba was exposed.

When King David saw Bathsheba bathing on the rooftop, he allowed his flesh to take over. He became under evil's influence, sinfully called another man's wife to his chambers, and there he lay with Bathsheba. The prophet Isaiah warns this woman who is complacent to be aware of the potential dangers around her.

> "Rise up, you women who are at ease, hear my voice; you complacent daughters, give ear to my speech." (Isaiah 32:9, ESV)

Whenever sin and worldly attitudes find their way into the presence of God's people, Satan will be in the midst of their lives. Being at ease with living an ungodly lifestyle destroys families. Now is the time to grieve and cry out to God. Ask Him to restore His favor through the transforming power of the Holy Spirit. Also, pray for the leaders, especially those who are under sinful influences. Ask God! Request that the leaders may have the benefits of spiritual salvation and a close relationship with Him through Jesus Christ.

Jesus' deepest desires for His followers are shown in His prayer recorded by the Apostle John in *John 17:1-26*. It is an example of how we should all pray for our leaders as well as those under our care. Jesus asked that God protect them from the evil influences of the world and keep them from turning away from Himself. He also asked for His followers to have discernment to recognize and reject ungodly beliefs. Let us follow Jesus' example and be prayerful for our leaders. Pray for those in high positions and those with authority.

> *Dear Holy Father,*
>
> *You gave your Son Jesus authority over all flesh, to give eternal life to all you have given Him.*
>
> *Thousands of leaders are actively working for kingdom sake. May you guard them so that no one will meet destruction. Sanctify them in the truth; your Word is truth. Since you have given them authority on earth, may they know and believe your truth. May they remain in your name and see the glory of Jesus. You are glorified to the highest. You are the only true God. In Jesus' name, I pray, Amen.*

Jesus used His God-given authority from His Father to righteously serve others and to free people from demonic control. From experience, Jesus knew and understood His Father. He recognized what God did for the world. He gave authority to His followers, but He didn't want His followers to become puffed up with pride.

Consequently, His followers were given command concerning their service to others. Those who accepted His teachings were warned not to be like the rulers and officials of the world who use their authority in a way that control others for selfish gain. They were to model after Him, serving other through unconditional love.

"They were amazed at his teaching, because his words had authority." (Luke 4:32, NIV)

Jesus called them (disciples) together and said, "You know that the rulers in this world lord it over their people, and officials flaunt their authority over those under them. But among you it will be different. Whoever wants to be a leader among you must be your servant, and whoever wants to be first among you must be the slave of everyone else. For the Son of Man came not to be served but to serve others and to give his life as a ransom for many." (Mark 10:42-45, NLT).

"Do nothing from selfish ambition or conceit, but in humility count others more significant than yourselves. Let each of you look not to his own interest, but also to the interest of others." (Philippians 2:3-4, NIV)

Part of the support we can give to our spiritual leader or leaders is prayer. Pray they would continue to rely on the Lord and seek His wisdom in guiding others. Regularly take time to recognize the contributions they make in our lives. Express an attitude of respect and appreciation. Let's not plant the seed of disloyalty by giving grievous reports to others about them; make it easy for them to lead us.

Meanwhile, let's keep in mind that Jesus Chris is the ultimate leader in control of God's kingdom and no man surpasses Him. Jesus is loving, humble, obedient, and selfless; this is the leader we must keep our eyes on. In doing so, the characters of those around you will be unveiled as one that is in need of a prayer or one that truly follows Jesus. The characteristics of those truly following Christ will manifest honor to the Lord. For that reason, they will be known as ones doing what Christ has asked of them: feeding His sheep.

CHAPTER 14

INSPIRINGLY SUBMISSIVE WOMEN

Their virtues are:
Heartening
   Encouraging
      Invigorating
         Effecting
            Uplifting
               Stimulating
                  Activating

The Bible gives reference to several women in their correct position of submission. Ruth, Esther, and Tabitha are a few who supported the ministry of the Bible. All of these women have something in common. They acknowledge, through God's word, that they are of the weakest vessel in a spiritual sense. They knew they could become a target of Satan at any given moment.

These women of God surrendered themselves to the authority of their male spiritual leaders as God had commanded them to do. They tolerated and accepted the influence over them with ease. All of the women mentioned in the Bible have been influenced and affected by the power of men in some way or another.

Important facts to consider would be how they performed in their role and how they reacted to these influences of the men. These women described in the Bible demonstrated their expressions only during appropriate times and they managed to remain in their position of submission to their leaders. Only under the grace of God was their presence able to fill the atmosphere with powerful energy. During performances of expressing their emotions, each woman's character suffered the same emotional issues on, a daily basis, just as modern-day women.

The virtuous woman is an inspiringly submission woman. She is modest and has a character of goodness and righteousness. She is one that Almighty God places in positions that will benefit His kingdom as well as her personal life. He places her in regard to the nature of her character. God finds delight in the admirable qualities of a virtuous woman. These qualities are also admired by her family and many people around her. She can practice these qualities by allowing her presence to reflect godly morals of a devout Christian.

The Book of Proverbs describes a virtuous woman as one not easily found, and her price is worth far more than rubies. She is not easily found in that she is not easily created. Only the Spirit of God has the power to produce such a creature. This woman is well protected by the Spirit of God because she is precious to Him; her footsteps are prevented from walking into harm and danger. Descriptions on the lifestyle of a virtuous woman are written in Proverbs 31:10-31.

- She is admired by many.
- She is one that God can use to benefit His kingdom.
- Her husband's heart has great trust in her.
- She gives her love and attention where it is needed.
- Her husband and her children are all blessed due to her good works.
- She is a wise woman.
- She is well aware of the power of God.
- She desires righteousness because this is pleasing to God.
- She is fed from her own goodness toward other people.
- Her heart's desire is to please God.
- Her motive is to remain in her correct position of submission.

VIRTUOUS WOMEN OF OLD

RUTH

In the Old Testament of the Bible, there are several women who brought glory to God's name. We have Ruth, a beautiful young Moabite who was a childless widow. Ruth and her mother-in-law, Naomi, suffered a terrible misfortune: the men in their family all died, including their husbands. Naomi decided to return to her hometown of Bethlehem and Ruth was determined to go with her and serve the God of Naomi's family.

Ruth wanted to be in the presence of Jehovah God and under His approval. Ruth's commitment to remain with her mother-in-law shows her submissiveness was voluntary and her enthusiasm to serve God was not tied to selfish motives. She knew Jehovah was a mighty God to serve and this is where she wanted to be. Bound together by their common grief, the two set off on the road to Bethlehem. Arriving at the gates of Bethlehem, Ruth severs her ties to Moab and embraces Naomi's family, her country, and her God.

> *"Ruth replied to Naomi, 'Don't urge me to leave you or to turn back from you. Where you go, I will go, and where you stay I will stay. Your people will be my people and your God my God.'" (Ruth 1:16, NIV)*

God saw Ruth as a determined woman; therefore, He allowed her to find and receive peace in Bethlehem. A direct intervention from God gave her peace and rest because her heart was sincere. Her rest was being placed under Boaz, her spiritual provider and protector.

Boaz called Ruth a "woman of noble character" because of her impressive qualities. He married Ruth and she gave birth to a son, Obed, which means "a servant who worships." Through her refuge and kindness, Ruth was able to be free of discomfort and disturbances of the world. Both human and divine examples of God show the excellence of our Redeemer.

> "And now, my daughter, don't be afraid. I will do for you all you ask. All the people of my town know that you are a woman of noble character." (Ruth 3:11, NIV)

Ruth deserved to become a part of the Jewish royal family, which would eventually produce the Messiah. She could be used by God to glorify His kingdom. Ruth became an ancestress of our Savior, as she was one of the women who gave birth to the sons in the line of David. This is the same line under which Jesus was born. We can see this example as an important power-driven point. When we are sincere at heart to serve God, with the right intentions and motive, we are in position to receive great blessings and benefits for ourselves as well as our family.

> Then Boaz announced to the elders and all the people, "Today you are witnesses that I have bought from Naomi all the property of Elimelek, Kilion and Mahlon. I have also acquired Ruth the Moabite, Mahlon's widow, as my wife, in order to maintain the name of the dead with his property so that the name will not disappear from among his family or from his hometown. Today you are witnesses." (Ruth 4:9-10, NIV)

From Ruth's outstanding qualities of faithfulness and loyalty, we learn certain virtues are the only foundation that brings true happiness in life. She also teaches us that racial hatred and religious bigotry are solved only through a relationship with our Creator. There is reward in our faithfulness. God looks deep inside of all people and He is fully engaged in shaping the future of the world.

ESTHER

Esther was a Jewish orphan, daughter of a Benjamite named Abihail. She lost her parents at an early age and Mordecai, her cousin, adopted her and became her father and spiritual leader. She lived under his protection in Persia, capital of Suza, a city filled with Jewish exiles.

In the book of Esther, she is recorded in the Bible as being beautiful and attractive. One command Mordecai gives to her is not to reveal to anyone that she is Jewish. Mordecai, being the chief minister of King Ahasuerus, knew someday Esther, being a virgin, would be called to the palace of King Ahasuerus. As ruler of the Persian Empire, he was in in search of a replacement queen.

> *"Mordecai had a cousin named Hadassah, whom he had brought up because she had neither father nor mother. This woman who was also known as Esther, had a lovely figure and was beautiful. Mordecai had taken her as his own daughter when her father and mother died." (Esther 2:7, NIV)*

> *"Esther had not revealed her nationality and family background, because Mordecai had forbidden her to do so." (Esther 2:10, NIV)*

Esther submits herself and is obedient to Mordecai as her spiritual leader. She appears to be cooperative to his authority and control. Because of God's grace, her beauty out measured all the other women, and she was kindly disposed by everyone in the palace, including King Ahasuerus. The king was attracted to Esther and she was highly favored over the other virgins. She won the king's approval and elegantly replaced Vashti as queen of Persia.

This favor was a gift from God to the Jewish people because of Esther's submissiveness to Him and to Mordecai. Her life and the life of the Jewish are the same in that her fate would have a lasting effect on the people. The king was disposed to be generous to Esther's people, as they needed an abundance of deliberation. She remained faithful and patiently waited for God's power to be displayed in the lives of the Jewish people. Her obedience gave her grace—she stood out above many other women.

> *"Now the king was attracted to Esther more than to any of the other women, and she won his favor and approval more than any of the other virgins. So, he set a royal crown on*

> her head and made her queen instead of Vashti." (Esther
> 2:17, NIV)

Here, we have another woman in her correct position of submission that glorifies God. Along with her obedience and faithfulness, Esther's grace and beauty served also as an advantage to the kingdom of God. The Lord was glorified as Esther and her family remained faithful to Him.

The king was so pleased with Esther, he accepted her request and he made the decision to help save Ester's people from the hands of a wicked man, Haman. This decision brought about the downfall of the Jewish enemy, Haman, who wanted to destroy and kill all the Jewish people. However, God's plan for His people can't be overthrown by a sinful and mischievous man.

> "The king asked, 'What is it Esther? What is your request?
> Even up to half the kingdom, it will be given to you.'"
> (Esther 5:3, NIV)

> "The king's edict granted the Jews in every city the right
> to assemble and protect themselves, to destroy, kill and
> annihilate the armed men of any nationality or province
> who might attack them and their women and children, and
> to plunder the property of their enemies." (Esther 8:11, NIV)

We must remember greatness is never found in riches or power; it is always found in our faithfulness and devotion to God. Esther was a not only a model for all the Jewish women living in exile, but she posed as a modern-day sculpture for all of us.

TABITHA

Tabitha is another woman the Bible describes as being submissive to God. The Apostle Luke, the writer of the book of Acts, presents her as a remarkable woman devoted to good works and acts of charity. She is described as being a disciple and dedicated to pleasing God. Tabitha was available for God to use and placed herself totally at His disposal. She was a positive influence on the females in the city of Joppa. The Holy Spirit worked through her acts of love and kindness.

Being an important pillar of the community, she was unique in that she was a symbol of Christ. She served the entire community of Joppa. Tabitha spent a lot of time showing love toward the widows and caring for them. Tabitha was a great inspiration to the females in the community. When she died, her death had such a profound impact on the women of Joppa. Her death was a sudden blow and the women grieved heavily for Tabitha. During these days, communities lost many good people to death.

> *"In Joppa, there was a disciple named Tabitha (in Greek her name is Dorcas); she was always doing good and helping the poor. About that time, she became sick and died, and her body was washed and placed in an upstairs room." (Acts 9:36-37, NIV)*

The Holy Spirit worked through the Apostle Peter to raise Tabitha from the dead. The Spirit of God allowed Peter exercised his supernatural powers to raise Tabitha back to life. She was the only adult woman chosen as one of seven people the Bible mentions being resurrected from the dead.

Tabitha's resurrection serves us two purposes. In one manner, it is an example of how mighty the power of God operates; and the kingdom of God will continue to be beneficial through Tabitha's good work. She is blessed with the opportunity to continue with her life on earth and utilize her spiritual abilities.

> *"Peter sent them all out of the room, then he got down on his knees and prayed. Turning toward the dead woman, he said, "Tabitha, get up." She opened her eyes, and seeing Peter she sat up. He took her by the hand and helped her to her feet. Then he called for the believers, especially the widows, and presented her to them alive." (Acts 9:40-41, NIV)*

LIFE OF A GODLY WOMAN

Sitting in a special room she dedicated to the Lord, she prayed avidly for hundreds of people. We talked about her in earlier chapters. Joy Harris spent most of her adult life serving the Lord. My mother made a personal choice to serve the Lord and brought every area of her life under submission to God's will. She realized submitting to God's will was the key to being, a godly woman.

She met our father, Louis Harris, in September 1955 and they were married three months later, on December 23, 1955. One of my dad's favorite songs to her was "Ninety-nine and a Half Won't Do" because he knew she was his hundred. As their children, we were able to witness respect, support, trust, friendship, and most of all, *love*. The love our parents had for each other only comes once in a lifetime.

While faced with the sinful influences of the world my mother remained faithful to God and followed Jesus in her everyday life. She constantly read God's Word until her eyesight weakened and she was no longer able to read, but she remained a listener. No matter the circumstances she remained faithful to the Lord because she knew He would work it out. Mom knew the wonderful affirmation of God's mercy, grace, and faithfulness. These things were more than often uttered.

Joy was also a humble woman who submitted herself to her husband as to the Lord for a glorious fifty-eight years. Mom was a quiet person and didn't have much to chatter about unless it was a subject pertaining to God and spiritual things. When she did speak, what she had to say was worth listening to because her conversation was always about God. She was compassionate and considerate of others. She helped many people in their walk with Jesus. Her mode of expression, told to everybody was, "God loves you." She was another one who brought glory to God's holy name.

Apart from these facts, she was also a prayer warrior for the Lord, interceding on behalf of others in this spiritual warfare. I retain in my memory waking up in the middle of the night, seeing her on her knees praying. God calls all believers to fight in the spiritual warfare, as battles are constantly taking place and evil is causing so much suffering. Many who say, "yes" to God's call are prayer warriors and they participate in the kingdom's most important work.

My mother had an elderly friend, Mrs. Hope, who was about ninety-years-old. They were close and spent a lot of time on the telephone praying. One day, an extremely bad thing happened to Mrs. Hope. She lived alone after her husband had passed away several years before. One night a man broke into her house, beat, robbed, and raped the elderly lady.

Mrs. Hope called and told her what happened. Mom immediately had dad to drive her to Mrs. Hope's house. My mom helped her to gather a few clothes and she brought Mrs. Hope back to our house. I can still remember mom sitting by the bedside of Mrs. Hope for months, nursing her until she regained some strength. I cried when my mom's friend left our house and went back home. Mom showed this same compassion to everyone with whom she came in contact.

On May 17, 2014, my mother passed away from metastatic breast cancer. It's an aggressive form of breast cancer and not easy treatable. Surgery and radiation were not enough to prevent the spread of the disease, which spread to her bones, liver, and brain. During the end, she lay six days in a coma, unable to speak or move with her family by her side. In, an effort to give her comfort, her children sat by the bedside and took turns reading Bible Scriptures to her and softly singing praises to God, which filled the room with a spiritual aroma.

We often wondered what had caused such a horrific thing to come upon our mother. The Bible reveals Satan as the cause of sickness and disease, including cancer. During Mom's last couple of days on earth, I witnessed Satan as he tried to use the suffering of her illness to draw her attention away from God. The devil made one final attempt to try to get her to relinquish her unwavering faith in God. The expression on mom's face showed she was in agony and needed help.

"When Jesus had called the twelve (disciples) together, he gave them authority to drive out all demons and cure diseases, and he sent them out to proclaim the kingdom of God and to heal." (Luke 9:1, ESV)

The highlight of the story is, this was a woman who had spent her whole life praying for others and now she needed a warrior. The last few minutes of her life were crucial, and she needed prayer. She needed someone to stand in the gap just as she had done for so many others. With encouragement, I reminded mother, saying, "Mom, God loves you and has never left your side. He is still with you right now. The same way He was with Jesus on that cross, He is with you. Satan has taken over your body, but he will not have your soul."

As I prayed over her and read the Scriptures from the Holy Bible aloud, I had come to Psalm 46, when the doorbell rang. I immediately got up and went to the door, opened it, and no one was there. We all instantly knew that the holy angels had come to assist this warrior in her journey home. I went back to her bedside and sensed there was a powerful presence in the room.

The reading of Scriptures and prayer continued; and the expression on mom's face began to change and show she was at peace again. A few minutes later, she lifted her hands in praise to God and gave Him the glory. She then took her last breath. The Lord had called, and she was gone. Mother spent over forty years enthusiastically praising God. Her favorite words were "God loves you" and she told these words to everybody. She was an inspiringly submissive woman and is greatly missed by many.

> "The Lord of Heaven's Armies is here among us; the God of Israel is our fortress." (Psalm 46:7, NLT)

> "In my distress, I prayed to the Lord, and the Lord answered me and set me free." (Psalm 118:5, NLT)

A godly woman is precious in God's sight and humble in nature. She is modest and seeks a good reputation. She knows that good works of Christians are only genuine when the soul of the performer is saturated with the works. She is mild mannered, has a pleasant personality, and her conversation is decent and becoming of a godly woman. If, by chance, her husband passes away before she does, she can rest assure that she is still covered with grace and dignity.

Our eyes should reflect the compassion of our Lord and Savior. Unselfish service to God's kingdom fills the earth with a peculiar scent, a fragrance that's satisfying to the spiritual part of humans. We too can be a vessel by living a life that glorifies God through acts of goodness and kindness in the name of Christ. Through the eyes of our creator, we are inspiringly submissive women.

THE WOMAN OF NOBLE CHARACTER

"An excellent wife who can find?
She is far more precious than jewels.
The heart of her husband trusts in her,
And he will have no lack of gain.
She does him good, and not harm, all the days of her life.
Her husband is known in the gates when he sits with the elders of the land.
She opens her mouth with wisdom, and the
teaching of kindness is on her tongue.
She looks to the ways of her household and
does not eat the bread of idleness.
Her children will rise up and call her blessed;
Her husband also, and he praises her:
Many women have done excellently,
But you surpass them all."
(Proverbs 31:10-12, 23, 26-29, ESV)

— CHAPTER 15 —

LONG-SHOTS TRAVEL WITH THE KING

Various theories exist why people willingly stake their values on the outcome of something involving a chance. Taking a risk on speculation goes back far in time and began in the United States during the 1600's. Some states in America have legalized  and call it gambling. The risk of taking one's hard-earned money and putting it up for bets is, to some people, a game of skills.

Gambling is big business and can be habit-forming. It is worldwide and popular at casinos, racetracks, and even some church halls. It is thought to bring revenue to a city and jobs to citizens. It has become an addiction for many as they continue to spend money they don't have. When it comes to mastering the win of slot machines, bingo, and long shots, this skill can incite a middle schooler.

To give an idea of what a long shot is, let's look at racehorses for a moment. In economics and gambling, a long-shot horse is given the odds of 50-to-1 and another 100-to-1 at winning in a race. According to the "rules of the house," pulling for a long shot is going against the odds. The term "rules of the house" was an earlier term used for management of the event. These rules govern the entire race and they are imperative to the game.

Most assuredly, I'm not a gambler, but I do watch live the televised Kentucky Derby held in Louisville, Kentucky annually. A long shot never fails to seize my attention during the race. The potential of these horses could shock the world with their wins. The gamblers betting on a long shot are, considered to be in a much worse proposition than betting on a favorite horse. Why? Because the odds are against this horse.

The winner of the 1918 Kentucky Derby, Exterminator, was an American Thoroughbred Hall of Fame racehorse that defied the odds. He won Horse of the Year with honors in 1922. The lanky chestnut colt was bred and foaled at Almahurst Farm near Lexington, Kentucky. Although awkward and coarse looking, the big colt grew fast, reaching 16.3 hands (sixty-seven inches, 170 cm) at two years of age.

During his traveling days, he raced until the age of nine, a relatively old age for a race horse. Many fans called him "Old Bones" or "The Galloping Hat rack" and among the stable lads, he was "Old Shang." Exterminator finished his duties and retired in 1924 to a life of grass and leisure, with a succession of companion ponies, all named Peanuts, at his side. He died at the age of thirty on September 26, 1945 and his grave is at Whispering Pines Pet Cemetery shared by fellow racehorses in Binghamton, New York.

A LONG-SHOT RUNNING

Let's take a look at our traveling days as a long shot. In traveling with the King, Jesus Christ, we are progressing from one stage of life to another. This is the stage where we go from a sentence of death to a promise of life. Long shots are required to always follow the "rules of the house," which is God's Word. In an effort to ensure the runner will have an opportunity at success, conforming to the Word of God is crucial. In order to oppose and withstand the trials of the devil, one must adhere to all spiritual principles.

All long shots committed to this adventure are involved in a notable degree of risks. The risks include being tempted to a large degree by the evil one. Still, the Lord promises great rewards if successful. Traveling with Jesus is an investment, even if you have little or no experience in conducting yourself in a particular manner. He still considers you great and worthy of compensation. The return of the investment is everlasting life in the heavenly places with our King, Jesus Christ.

*"And lead us not into temptations, but deliver us from the
evil one." (Matthew 6:13, NIV)*

The enemy of Jesus considers long shots to be a bad proposition
because he thinks his demons will defeat the long shots. Jesus was a long
shot; many regarded Him as a loser and they refrained from believing He
was the Son of God, including some of the Jewish people. The people
thought Jesus didn't have a fighting chance against the ordinary customs
of the Roman governor, Pontius Pilate. Then there is the devil who
appeared to Jesus on several occasions in an attempt to pressure every
circumstance and throw Him off track.

Jesus defeated Satan by destroying the works of evil as He performed
miracles on people and cast out demons. When the Lord Jesus died on
the cross, it seemed to Satan as if the powers of death were victorious.
Still, Jesus victoriously rose from the grave over Satan and the powers
of darkness.

Christ continues to defeat the enemy through the lives of long shots
and ordinary people. These are believers who have been delivered from
the kingdom of darkness and transformed into the kingdom of light.
Some of them are ones the enemy thought wouldn't make it to eternal
life with Jesus. These are the believers who will not give up and will
finish with lifelong measures of endurance.

*"God anointed Jesus of Nazareth with the Holy spirit and
power, and how he went around doing good and healing all
who were under the power of the devil, because God was
with him." (Acts 10:38, NIV)*

Today, every man and woman have an honorable opportunity to
please God by getting in our correct position of the race. Finding our
spiritual position before the race certainly puts a smile on the face of
our Lord. May we run with the spirit of a long shot, having a measurable
degree of endurance to the finish line, which is physical death. May we
retire to an eternal life of grass and leisure with our Lord, Jesus Christ.

> "Carefully determine what pleases the Lord. Take no part
> in the worthless deeds of evil and darkness; instead expose
> them. It is shameful even to talk about the things that
> ungodly people do in secret." (Ephesians 5:10-12, NLT)

Jesus, being in a position of authority, in God's view He is held responsible for the spiritual wellbeing of all believers. This person placed in charge of others always has extensive duties to uphold. These obligations stretch all the way from protection to discipline. They record the outcome of each individual standing in the line of long shots. Jesus realizes in some ways God is holding Him accountable.

Another long shot chosen by God was Ezekiel. God placed Ezekiel in a position of authority over Israel. He was in submission to God at the same time responsible for the lives of the people of Israel. He provided safety and protection for the people. His authority over Israel means that He will be the influence that will have a changing effect on God's people. This is through the information and laws he receives from God. Ezekiel has power by God to enforce these laws because the house of Israel is disobedient. (See Ezekiel 3:16-27).

Upon receiving his duties, Ezekiel has, to perform his responsibility to the people just as God instructed. If the job is not from beginning to end and according to instructions, the people may not get clear understanding of the will of God. Some may not know a message or warning is in place; as a result of being blind, the people will continue to live sinful lives. If this happens, the blood of the people will be on the hands of Ezekiel because he is responsible for their spiritual wellbeing.

All individuals appointed by God in a leadership position have the same responsibility to protect those they guide. Each one serving in a leader's position must answer directly to Christ. There are several others the Bible mentions as having authority by God for a particular purpose: Jesus Christ, Daniel, Hosea, Joel, Amos, Obadiah, Jonah, Micah, Nahum, Habakkuk, Zephaniah, Haggai, Zechariah, Malachi, John the Baptist, the twelve apostles, also many more.

They were placed in position of authority to carry out the plan God had designed. Some of them quickly moved into position as ordered with no hesitations; and the spirit of rebellion was not present. They knew the power and sovereignty of God and this allowed them to adopt an attitude of submission. As an outcome, their knowledge of God gave them the desire to embrace their obedience to God.

On the other hand, some were not-so-willing to accept their assigned position and rebelled against the order given to them. They ran or tried to run away from the responsibility that God placed on them. They hesitated and were reluctant because they were not willing to perform the duties. Many moved at a snail's pace as if they were in control of time. They did not immediately comply with God's order. This is a form of insubordination and rebellion, simply because they opposed the instructions.

JESUS CHRIST WILLINGLY SUBMITS

As we know, Jesus Christ is the perfect example of one who submitted to God and willingly accepted His assignment. He immediately moved into position and began His journey. He did all that was required of Him. Jesus stated several times who He was and who sent Him. He often mentioned the reason why He was here on earth.

> "For I have come down from heaven, not to do my own will but to do the will of him that sent me". (John 6:38-40)

Jesus said He came from Heaven and He came here to Earth to do the will of the one that sent Him here. He mentioned He came here not to do His own will. A will is an action that determines the intentions of someone exercising power. Jesus mentioned He was here to do His Father's will. He has authorization from God to carry out the intentions of His Father.

In John 4:34, Jesus explains His food, or his meat is to do the will of His Father. Jesus does not hunger for anything earthly. His hunger is to do the work elected for Him to do. For Jesus, constantly doing His job on earth, is what kept Him full, until His father called Him home. He will continue this feeding until His assignment is complete.

Jesus finished His assignment and said to God, "I have finished the work you gave me" (John 17:4, ESV). He reported to His Father without grief because His job was accomplished well. Part of the job was to glorify His Father.

> *"And lo a voice from heaven saying, 'this is my beloved Son in whom I am well pleased.'" (Matthew 3:17)*

Matthew tells us that the voice of God spoke from heaven saying that He was well pleased with his Son, Jesus. God spoke these words many years before Jesus finished his assignment on Earth. God was well pleased with Jesus because even before the point of Jesus' baptism, Jesus had already shown he was interested in submitting to God. He had already shown that He was doing what God asked of Him. Jesus received a good evaluation. What an awesome example for you and me to follow.

JONAH, STUBBORN AND REBELLIOUS

Jonah is a perfect example of one that did not immediately move into position that God assigned to him. He was not willing to submit to his assignment and his actions showed a behavior of rebellion.

In reading the book of Jonah, we can see that God gave him specific instructions. He instructed him to go to a specific city and give orders to a particular group of people. These people of that particular city had become involved in major wickedness. God chose Jonah to handle this task and only Jonah.

As we read on, Jonah mentions how he rebelled against the order of God and that he was not willing to do what God had set apart for him to do. He was noncompliant and instead of obeying the command of God, Jonah ran to a different place. He was trying to hide from God because he knew God was not going to accept his rebellion. See Jonah 1:1-15.

> *"Then the Lord spoke to Jonah a second time: 'Get up and go to the great city of Nineveh, and deliver the message I have given you.' This time Jonah obeyed the Lord's command and went to Nineveh, a city so large it took three days to see it all." (Jonah 3:1-3, NLT)*

After Jonah experienced the repercussions of his disobedience, he surrendered and with his whole heart, he prayed to God. He knew God was not going to accept his rebellion. God answered his prayer and Jonah accepted the assignment God had given him. Now he realizes he has a great responsibility and will be accountable for the lives of many people. He must report to God for their souls. Jonah's submissiveness produced great results. All parties involved received assistance including him. Again, an advantage to the kingdom of God was achieved.

FINDING OUR POSITION

Whether we are leading a group of people or actively working alongside other Christians we are traveling with the King. Having faith in God is key to finding our position. The appropriate position maybe as male leader or female leader, one who counsels and supervises those ones who turn their attention to leaders for assistance. This position may be as a husband, or as a wife, who is directly under a husband's supervision with him managing her everyday life.

On the other hand, the correct position may be to remain single, but under a pastor and spiritual leaders who are helping to guide while traveling this road. This position is maintained while remaining under the leadership of those who are authorized to supervise through our Lord Jesus Christ. In either case, the Spirit of God controls through the links of spiritual earthly leaders.

The life of each individual man and woman is on exhibit to be viewed, because all are under the same supreme authority of Almighty God. No matter which position we're in, whether as leader or as apprentice, we can be confident that we have the same opportunity to receive massive amounts of grace, as did the Apostle Paul. May we live a peaceful and quiet life, one that is godly and dignified, worthy of traveling with our Lord Jesus Christ.

- If we are not sure of the right place to be,
- If we have a stubborn streak which prevents us from moving
- Grace will see you through.

Grace and hope is always available to assist us in getting there. A prayer in the book of Psalms can be used as a wonderful guide. We can approach God and ask Him to place us in a position that He sees fit. Allowing the Holy Spirit to move us into our proper dwelling place is an act of submission. *(See Psalm 26:1-12.)*

REMAINING IN PLACE

In order to continue in a character of moral excellence, it takes dedication and determination. There must be a decision made to do God's will along with a serious commitment. Our own will must be to do the will of God. After this decision is made, there must be time and attention set aside for the sole purpose of developing a strong attachment to pleasing God.

Through our prayers and worship, we are showing affection and enthusiasm to God and His kingdom. Our continued interest in Him is what keeps us in our place of submission. If we keep our attention directed toward the Lord, peace will always be with us and obstacles are easy to overcome. Peace gives us the incentive to remain in our proper place of submission.

During the most stressful days on our planet, there will be intervals of trouble, but we must continually strive to keep our focus on the Lord. The trials are only temporary; they cause our faith to grow and give glory to God. The prophet Isaiah tells us that we can find the needed strength to continue the road to a successful spiritual life.

> *"You will keep in perfect peace those whose minds are steadfast, because they trust in you. Trust in the Lord forever, for the Lord, the Lord God himself, if the Rock eternal." (Isaiah 26:3-4, NIV)*

In addition to keeping our mind upon the Lord, hard work and determination pushes forth an admirable character that is pleasing to God. It's been over fifty years and I, the little six-year-old girl, am living proof that all shifts in life are for our benefit and training purposes. The experiences we encounter provide us with an opportunity to make corrections, move back into our correct position, and submit to God's order. The Lord then brings us back to where we belong: to God.

Today, I remain in the appreciation phrase giving thanks to God, Jesus Christ, and the Holy Spirit for many things. Thanking Jehovah God for His wisdom and for giving me a desire to serve Him. I will always be grateful for the overcrowded bedroom, the limited space, the strict rules, and the critters, too. They were all a part of the training program. The praise, honor, and glory of it all belong to the Lord.

Satan's delusion has always been that he is like God. We as Christians know that to be false. The enemy has made his way into peoples' lives and some churches inserting false teachings and convincing believers to sin against God. He has hurt many people and destroyed several families, but his end will come. His authority over the earth and power of mankind will end in a massive war and judgment. One the world has never experienced. His final doom will be when he is destroyed and thrown into the lake of burning sulfur.

> "And the devil who had deceived them was thrown into the lake of fire and sulfur where the beast and the false prophet were, and they will be tormented day and night forever and ever." (Revelation 20:10, ESV)

We are all individually equipped with the potential of being lovely children of God. Be confident that the desires of our heart toward him are unmovable. Make sure our love buckets do not remain empty or stay full. Our faith in God is on display for all to see that we serve an awesome God. Let's all make sure our listening ears, spoken words, seeing eyes, and thoughts remain on the path to righteousness. At the end of the day, God still rules over all.

May your stride always be as the perfect model, Jesus Christ with your heart focused solely on the kingdom. May your spirit bring forth its lost memory that you belong to God and will forever be connected to Him and only Him. May God's Holy Spirit continue to keep you peacefully and submissively under His authority. Then you shall witness the wonders of God's power and enjoy His presence. May our passion and purpose always be in submission to glory for Jehovah God.

"Therefore, we do not lose heart. Though outwardly we are wasting away, yet inwardly we are being renewed day by day. For our light and momentary troubles are achieving for us an eternal glory that far outweighs them all. So, we fix our eyes not on what is seen, but on what is unseen, since what is seen is temporary, but what is unseen is eternal."
(2 Corinthians 4:16-18, NIV)

"Even though I walk through the darkest valley,
I will fear no evil, for you are with me,
your rod and your staff, they comfort me.
You prepare a table before me in the presence of my enemies.
You anoint my head with oil, my cup overflows.
Surely your goodness and love will follow me all the days of
my life, and I will dwell in the house of the Lord forever."
(Psalm 23:4-5, NIV)

PRAY FOR A SUBMISSIVE ATTITUDE

O Lord, I thank you for revealing my complete plan through your Word. Thank you that I am delivered from the insubordinate spirit. Help me to become the woman who quickly chooses humility, give me the quality of being discreet. Let the heart of my husband trusts me completely, have me to do him good all the days of my life. Allow me to see the glory of thy lasting joy. Holy, holy, holy are you, everlasting Lord. Amen!

PRAY FOR SPIRITUAL CLEANSING

(Example prayer is taken from Psalm 51:1-15, KJV).
Dear Father, Hear my prayer
Oh God, please have mercy upon me according to your loving kindness.
Give ear to the words of my mouth.
Today, I acknowledge that I have sinned against you, by being in the midst of evil conditions and situations.
Purge me with hyssop, cleanse me of all undesirable traits so that I may be white as snow.

Please, create in me a clean heart, renew a right spirit within me so, that my behavior may be righteously pleasing to you.
Continue to construct my spirit daily into perfect righteousness.
I will teach your ways to others who have also gone beyond the boundary line set by you.
I pray these many things in your Son, Christ Jesus' name, Amen.

PRAY FOR OUR LEADERS

Dear Holy Father,
   You gave your son Jesus authority over all flesh, to give eternal life to all you have given him. Thousands of leaders are actively working for kingdom sake. May you guard them so that no one will meet destruction. Sanctify them in the truth, your word is truth. Since you have given them authority on earth may they know and believe your truth. May they remain in your name and see the glory of Jesus. You are glorified to the highest. You are the only true God. In Jesus' name, I pray, Amen.

WOMAN OF NOBLE CHARACTER

"An excellent wife who can find?
She is far more precious than jewels.
The heart of her husband trusts in her,
and he will have no lack of gain.
She does him good, and not harm, all the days of her life. ...
Her husband is known in the gates when he sits with the elders of the land. ...
She opens her mouth with wisdom, and the teaching of kindness is on her tongue.
She looks to the ways of her household and does not eat the bread of idleness.
Her children will rise up and call her blessed;
her husband also, and he praises her:
Many women have done excellently,
But you surpass them all."
(Proverbs 31:10-12, 23, 26-29, ESV)

SOURCES

Schoenian, Susan. *Sheep 202, A Beginner's Guide to Raising Sheep.* 2011.
http://www.sheep101.info/201/behavior.html

Ludwig van Beethoven

Salter, Hanna, The biography of Ludwig van Beethoven 2017
http://www.lvbeethoven.com/Bio/BiographyLudwig.html

Hibbert, Christopher. "The Rise and Fall of the Medici Bank." *History Today* Volume 24 Issue, August 8, 1974 http://www.historytoday.com/christopher-hibbert/rise-and-fall-medici-bank

"The Medici Family." http://themedicifamily.com/The-Medici-Bank.html 2017

Baker, 1987 "Even When He's Silent." Stories for Preaching. God on the Witness Stand https://storiesforpreaching.com/category/sermonillustrations/doubt/

Pope Benedict XVI, May 28, 2006, "In This Place of Horror." http://www.historyplace.com/speeches/pope-benedict-auschwitz.htm

Smoltczyk, Alexander, May 29, 2006, Spiegel Magazine "German Silence in Auschwitz." http://www.spiegel.de/international/spiegel/pope-benedict-xvi-in-poland-german-silence-in-auschwitz-a-418593.html

Famous peace speech quoted: https://www.youtube.com/watch?v=7BEhKgoA86U

Kennedy, John F. "Peace & Inspirational Quotes." The Peace Alliance. 2016 http://peacealliance.org/tools-education/peace-inspirational-quotes/?gclid=CNXNp-KuqdECFZa6wAodebgK3w

Mandela, Nelson. "Peace & Inspirational Quotes." The Peace Alliance. 2016 http://peacealliance.org/tools-education/peace-inspirational-quotes/?gclid=CNXNp-KuqdECFZa6wAodebgK3w

History.com Staff 2009, http://www.history.com/topics/nelson-mandela

Lama, Dalai. "Peace & Inspirational Quotes." The Peace Alliance. 2017 http://peacealliance.org/tools-education/peace-inspirational-quotes/?gclid=CNXNp-KuqdECFZa6wAodebgK3w

Hayes, Ron, April 13, 2015 Corter Consulting "The Great Manager You Need is Probably a Woman." http://corter.com/the-great-manager-you-need-is-probably-a-woman/

Definition of curiosity is from www.dictionary.com

US Food & Drug Administration, United States Department of Health and Human Resources, August 2012 "Guidance for Industry: Suicidal Ideation and Behavior: Prospective Assessment of Occurrence in Clinical Trials."http://www.fda.gov/drugs/guidancecomplianceregulatoryinformation/guidances/ucm315156.htm

McLaughlin, Elliott C., Sara Sidner, and Michael Martinez, "Oklahoma City cop convicted of rape sentenced to 263 years in prison," CNN January 22, 2016 http://www.cnn.com/2016/01/21/us/oklahoma-city-officer-daniel-holtzclaw-rape-sentencing/

Long-shot horse, Exterminator:

McGraw Eliza, The New York Times, A Long Shot to Remember 2017 https://therail.blogs.nytimes.com/2013/05/02/exterminator-a-long-shot-to-remember/

ABOUT THE AUTHOR

As a Christian, Trish loves nothing more than to help inspire and develop the potential in other people and her interests are far more of a spiritual aspect. She has an overpowering love for the Lord and recognizes He is the reason for her inspiration. Prior to submitting her life to Christ, she spent several years fighting the influential forces that almost destroyed her life both spiritually and physically.

With enthusiasm, Trish lives to tell her story of redemption. She and her husband Brian live in a suburb of Dallas, Texas and are active members of Parkway Hills Baptist Church in Plano. She enjoys the exposure of being involved with the women's ministry and devotes much of her time to the studies of spirituality and helping others.

Printed in the United States
By Bookmasters